TRINA HAHNEMANN

The
Scandinavian
Cookbook

PHOTOGRAPHY BY LARS RANEK

QUADRILLE

EDITORIAL DIRECTOR Anne Furniss
ART DIRECTOR Helen Lewis
PROJECT EDITOR Jenni Muir
PHOTOGRAPHER Lars Ranek
DESIGNER Vibeke Kaupert, www.kaupert.dk
ASSISTANT DESIGNER Katherine Case
PRODUCTION Vincent Smith, Marina Asenjo

First published in 2008 by
Quadrille Publishing Limited
Alhambra House, 27-31 Charing Cross Road, London WC2H 0LS
www.quadrille.co.uk

Cataloguing-in-Publication Data: a catalogue record for this book
is available from the British Library.

ISBN 978 184400 613 7
Printed in China

SCANDINAVIA IS A SMALL CORNER OF THE WORLD. It is inhabited by about 16 million people. Their daily lives are affected importantly by shifting seasons and changing weather patterns. Summer days are long and there is a lot of light, while winter days are cold and very dark.

This has a major impact on people's lives and, of course, on the way we cook. For this book I have tried to portray the contemporary Scandinavian kitchen and mixed it with the way that I personally like to cook. It is based on the seasons, as all good cooking must be, and presented month by month to inspire you to try some recipes from the Scandinavian tradition.

IT IS MY DREAM that people will take the time necessary in their daily lives to sit down and have a nice meal together. The food should be made out of the best, preferably organic, ingredients. It should be prepared with great care and love – without spending a whole day in the kitchen. And when the meal is ready it is an opportunity for us all to sit down together and exchange opinions, share our feelings, and to pass on bits of information on everyday matters. This opportunity should not be missed.

I still strongly believe that you should try to buy as much local produce as you can so that your diet evolves with the seasons. This also gives you something delicious to look forward to, because there is always a new season just around the corner. Summer will bring strawberries, new potatoes and fresh salad; autumn apples, game and mushrooms; winter cod, oysters and lobster; and when you just cannot eat any more root vegetables, spring will arrive and it will be time for fresh herbs, rhubarb and asparagus.

WHEN WRITING A COOKBOOK for people who are probably not familiar with the culinary tradition, methods and produce of my part of the world, I am faced with the challenge of translating a culture. There are so many things when we cook and eat that are implicit in our culture and that we take completely for granted. Even if we have never cooked or baked according to any specific recipe, we tend to know how our national dishes are made and how they should taste, because they have been passed down through the generations. Food is one of the best ways to exchange cultures without looking at politics or other divergences. Differences in food and cooking are less easily lost in translation. We can just meet as peoples and share some of the gifts this planet has given us: wonderful food, and a tradition of cultivating it in an infinite number of ways depending on our situation in life.

IF I THINK ABOUT SOME OF THE BEST MOMENTS OF MY LIFE, they usually involve sitting around a large table with friends and family, enjoying wonderful food and a nice glass of wine or beer, and talking of something important. I hope to have translated some of these moments into this book and tempted you to do the same – that is, to venture out into the Scandinavian kitchen and make it part of your everyday cooking.

Enjoy.

Trina Hahnemann

January

In winter it is dark for most of the day. The sky is so low that it seems as though you could reach out and touch it. Daylight disappears so quickly that on some days you do not even notice whether it was there. Breakfast seems to take on a new significance at this time of year.

Twenty years ago I moved away from Denmark for a while to live in London with my family. We celebrated my son's first birthday in London! In Denmark, it is a tradition to have a big breakfast on your birthday, and parents have to go to the bakery very early, prepare a big breakfast spread and surprise you. I did not have a baker nearby, so there was only one solution: I had to make the Danish pastries myself. It was not a bad idea, because the pastries turned out beautifully, and it has subsequently become a tradition in our family that I make homemade Danish pastries for everybody's birthday.

Homemade Danish pastries (Makes 25)

PASTRY DOUGH
25g fresh yeast
150ml lukewarm water
1 egg, beaten
1 tbsp caster sugar
½ tsp salt
325g plain wheat flour
250g cold butter, thinly sliced

FILLING
1 vanilla pod
250ml single cream
2 egg yolks
2 tbsp caster sugar
1 tbsp cornflour

ICING
(optional)
150g icing sugar
3 tbsp cocoa powder
hot water

FIRST PREPARE THE PASTRY. In a mixing bowl, dissolve the yeast in the water. Stir in the egg, sugar and salt. Add the flour and stir until the dough comes together and leaves the edge of the bowl. Turn it onto a floured work surface and knead for 5 minutes until it is shiny but not sticky. Put the dough back in the bowl, cover with cling film and leave to rise in the refrigerator for 15 minutes. Roll out the dough into a 50cm square. Spread the thin slices of butter over the dough about 10cm in from the edge, so that the square of dough has a smaller square of butter on top. Fold the corners of the dough over the butter so that they meet in the centre, making a square parcel.

CAREFULLY ROLL THE DOUGH into a 40 x 60cm rectangle, making sure that it doesn't crack and that the butter stays inside the dough parcel. Next you want to fold the dough so that the butter becomes layered within it. Fold the bottom third of dough over the middle third, and fold the top third down over that. Roll out the dough again and fold the same way. Put the dough in the refrigerator for 15 minutes, then repeat the rolling and folding process three times, remembering to let the dough rest in the refrigerator for 15 minutes each time.

PREPARE THE FILLING. Cut the vanilla pod in half lengthways and scrape out the seeds with the tip of a knife. Put the vanilla seeds and cream in a saucepan and bring to the boil. Meanwhile, beat the egg yolks and sugar together until the mixture is pale and fluffy, then stir in the cornflour. Pour a little bit of the hot cream into the egg mixture to temper it, then pour all of the egg mixture into the saucepan. Return the pan to a reduced heat and whisk until the custard starts to thicken. Take care not to let the custard boil, and beat continuously in order to avoid scorching. Remove from the heat and leave to cool before use.

ROLL OUT THE DOUGH to a 50cm square, then cut it into five rows of 10cm squares. Place 2 tsp of the filling on each square. Take each square's corners and fold them into the middle over the filling, pressing the edges together to seal. Turn each pastry upside down and place them on a baking tray lined with baking paper. Cover with a tea towel and leave to rise for 20 minutes at room temperature. Preheat the oven to 225°C (Gas 7). Brush the pastries with a little beaten egg and bake them for 12–15 minutes, then leave to cool on a wire rack.

TO MAKE THE ICING (if wanted), mix the icing sugar and cocoa powder together in a bowl, adding a little bit of hot water, and whisk to give a smooth, dark brown paste. Place a spoonful of the icing on each pastry and leave to set for 10 minutes before serving.

Rye bread is the traditional bread of Scandinavia and varies from region to region. We eat it for lunch and sometimes breakfast. When I was a child, my grandfather would make me a sandwich with a slice of white bread and a slice of rye bread with cheese in the middle. That was my favourite! To make rye bread, you need a sourdough, but you only have to make it once if you remember to save a bit of dough for next time before baking. The spelt buns below are my favourite morning buns.

Rye bread *(Makes 1 large loaf)*

STEP 1: THE SOURDOUGH
220g rye flour
300ml buttermilk
1 tsp coarse sea salt

STEP 2: THE DOUGH
750ml lukewarm water
375g rye flour
375g plain wheat flour
1 tbsp sea salt

STEP 3: THE LOAF
500g cracked whole rye
250ml lukewarm water
2 tsp salt

STEP 1: Mix the rye flour, buttermilk and salt in a bowl. Cover with foil and leave for 3 to 4 days at room temperature (25–30°C). And there you have a sourdough! But note that if the temperature is too low, the sourdough will not develop and instead will go bad.

STEP 2: In a large bowl, dissolve the sourdough in the lukewarm water. Add the rye flour, wheat flour and salt and stir with a wooden spoon until you have a runny dough. Cover the bowl with a tea towel and set aside for 12 hours at room temperature. I normally do this around dinner time so that it can sit overnight, then I can do step 3 the next morning.

STEP 3: Add the cracked whole rye, lukewarm water and salt to the dough and stir again with a wooden spoon until the rye grains are evenly distributed. Now take 3 tablespoons of the dough, add 2 tablespoons of coarse salt, and save in a container in the refrigerator ready for the next time you make rye bread. It will last there for up to 8 weeks. Remember to do this every time you make rye bread and you will not need to make the sourdough again.

POUR THE REST OF THE DOUGH into a non-stick loaf tin measuring 10cm wide x 29cm long x 9cm deep. (If you do not have a non-stick loaf tin, grease the inside with a little oil.) Cover the tin with a tea towel and leave the bread to rise for 3–6 hours, or until it has reached the rim of the tin. Preheat the oven to 175°C (Gas 3) and bake the loaf for 1 hour and 45 minutes. When it is done, take it out of the tin immediately and let it cool on a wire rack.

Spelt buns *(Makes 20)*

50g fresh yeast
400ml lukewarm water
400ml yoghurt
4 tbsp honey
800g wholemeal spelt flour
1 tbsp salt
1 beaten egg
poppy seeds, to sprinkle

DISSOLVE THE YEAST IN THE WATER, then add the yoghurt and honey. Sift the spelt flour and salt together and stir thoroughly into the yeast mixture. Leave to stand for about 5 minutes.

TIP THE DOUGH ONTO A FLOURED WORK SURFACE and knead well. Return the dough to the bowl, cover with a tea towel and leave to rise for 1 hour at room temperature.

PREHEAT THE OVEN to 200°C (Gas 6). Dust your hands with some flour and shape the dough into 20 small buns (the dough will be a bit sticky). Put the buns on oven trays lined with baking paper. Lightly glaze the buns with the beaten egg and sprinkle with poppy seeds. Bake for 30 minutes then leave them to cool on a wire rack.

Open sandwiches, made with rye bread, are preferably served with aquavit and beer. In the old days people ate very simple ones, such as rye bread with a slice of cold meat, and took them to work as a packed lunch. In the early twentieth century, decorated smørrebrød became fashionable as a late dinner, after theatre, or in dance restaurants where the guests did not want to spend hours sitting down to a meal and instead wanted to spend their time dancing. Smørrebrød are delicious and luxurious but do not take a lot of time to eat.

Smørrebrød: Open sandwich with plaice, prawns and basil dressing *(Serves 4)*

20 basil leaves, finely shredded
3 parsley sprigs, leaves only, finely chopped
1 tbsp lime juice
200ml full-fat crème fraîche
salt and pepper
40g rye flour
4 large plaice fillets
butter, for frying
4 slices rye bread
100g mixed leaves
100g frozen Greenland prawns, defrosted
1 lime, cut into 4 wedges

COMBINE THE BASIL, PARSLEY AND LIME JUICE in a bowl, then fold in the crème fraîche. Season with salt and freshly ground pepper and place in the refrigerator.

MIX THE RYE FLOUR WITH SOME SALT AND PEPPER and use this mixture to coat the plaice fillets. In a frying pan, melt a little butter and fry the fillets for 4 minutes on each side.

PLACE THE SLICES OF RYE BREAD ON A SERVING DISH. Divide the leaves among the bread slices then put a warm plaice fillet and some basil crème on each one. Top with the prawns and a lime wedge. Serve immediately, so the plaice is still warm. Cold beer is an excellent accompaniment.

Some dishes are best as plain and simple as possible. Whole plaice fried in butter and served with lemon and parsley potatoes: that is simple and tasty!

Pan-fried plaice with potatoes in parsley *(Serves 4)*

800g fingerling potatoes
salt and pepper
4 whole plaice
150g plain wheat or rye flour
125g butter
30g parsley, finely chopped

TO SERVE
1 lemon, sliced
dill sprigs

BOIL THE POTATOES IN A LARGE PAN of salted water until tender, then drain. Once they are cool enough to handle, peel them.

RINSE THE PLAICE IN COLD WATER, then coat each one in the flour, patting off the excess. Melt 75g of the butter in a frying pan and fry the fish for 5 minutes on each side. Keep the cooked fish warm while you fry the remainder.

MELT THE REMAINING BUTTER in a casserole. Add the peeled potatoes and let them fry a little before adding the parsley. Season with some salt and freshly ground pepper. Serve the plaice immediately with the potatoes, the sliced lemon and the dill sprigs.

Norwegian smoked salmon is world famous and tastes great, but salmon also tastes fabulous when marinated rather than smoked. The taste becomes light and in the recipe below it takes on a deep citrus flavour. The fresh salmon needs to be marinated for a few days before being frozen overnight. If you want to serve only six people at a time, divide the salmon into four batches and freeze them separately. You can use the salmon in hors d'oeuvres or sandwiches, or serve it as a light dinner or a starter in a three-course meal.

Marinated salmon *(Serves 20–24)*

1 organic orange
1 organic lemon
300g caster sugar
300g sea salt
1 side of salmon, filleted

TO SERVE
1 organic orange
1 organic lemon
toasted bread
green salad

IF YOU HAVE A ZESTER, use it to remove the zest from the orange and lemon because it will look fresh and tasty. Alternatively, finely grate the zest from the fruit. Mix the zests with the sugar and salt.

USE TWEEZERS TO REMOVE ANY PIN-BONES FROM THE SALMON FILLET. Spread the zest-sugar-salt mixture evenly over the entire surface of the salmon, then wrap it in cling film and leave for 3 days in a refrigerator.

AFTER 3 DAYS, TAKE THE SALMON OUT OF THE REFRIGERATOR, remove the cling film and wipe off the marinade with a paper towel. Wrap the salmon in cling film and freeze it for 12 hours, then take it out of the freezer and defrost it.

PUT THE SALMON ON A BOARD AND CUT IT INTO THIN SLICES with a very sharp knife. The traditional cutting technique starts diagonally at one corner of the salmon, and then works back toward the centre of the filet.

TO SERVE, remove the zest from the remaining orange and lemon and sprinkle it over the salmon, which you eat accompanied by toasted bread and a fresh green salad.

In the past 10 years it has become fashionable to serve root vegetables, and star chefs use them creatively in their menus. I think they are very important in our daily day diet as well. They are healthy and tasty, can be prepared in a thousand ways and eaten for lunch, in a salad, or as a side dish or garnish at dinner.

Chicken with root vegetables *(Serves 6)*

8 garlic cloves
1 fairly large organic chicken
salt and pepper
1 celeriac, peeled and cut into medium-sized cubes
3 beetroot, peeled and cut into medium-sized cubes
2 carrots, peeled and cut into medium-sized cubes
1 small handful fresh thyme
2 tbsp olive oil

TO SERVE
green salad
fresh bread

PREHEAT THE OVEN to 200°C (Gas 6). Put six of the garlic cloves inside the chicken and sprinkle it with salt and freshly ground pepper. Place the chicken in an ovenproof dish and roast for 40 minutes.

MEANWHILE, FINELY CHOP THE REMAINING GARLIC CLOVES and mix with the vegetables, thyme, olive oil and some salt and pepper.

AFTER 40 MINUTES, TAKE THE CHICKEN OUT OF THE OVEN and lift it out of the ovenproof dish. Spread the vegetables out evenly in the dish, place the chicken back on top and return to the oven to roast for another 30 minutes.

WHEN THE CHICKEN IS DONE, CUT IT INTO EIGHT PIECES and serve with the vegetables, a green salad and some bread.

February

Cross-country skiing in Norway is a hushed and beautiful experience. You go on skis into the mountains with a rucksack containing sandwiches and warm tea on your back. You ski long slopes, you do not have to queue up, and you are never run over. It is only you and the skis. Everything is so quiet, you can just focus and let your skis cut through the snow. It is hard work and perfect exercise, and when you come home the afternoon sauna or a long hot bath awaits. And hopefully some more lovely food.

The northern tip of Denmark is a magnificent place. The light is very special due to the sea's reflections in the sky, which make the light seem to come from all corners of the world. The mountains of southern Norway shelter the sky over Skagen and somehow cleanse the air. Huge sand dunes line the coast in the form of a large arrow pointing north. Two different seas, coming from east and west respectively, meet at the tip, where the currents clash, divide and return again in an eternal battle, leaving a long sand bar in between that keeps shifting position. Artists have been drawn to Skagen from all over Scandinavia for generations. Many famous dishes have therefore developed in this area and this is one of its famous fish soups.

Skagen fish soup (Serves 4)

FISH STOCK

1kg fish bones, from flat fish
1 garlic clove
1 onion
1 leek
1 carrot
1 large ripe tomato
2 tbsp olive oil
200ml dry white wine
3 bay leaves
10 whole black peppercorns
1 tbsp salt
2 litres water

SOUP

100ml dry white wine
1 tbsp lemon juice
200ml double cream
½ tsp saffron strands
1 leek, thinly sliced
1 carrot, cut into small cubes
200g crayfish tails
12 giant prawns
100g salmon fillet
100g pollack fillet
salt and pepper
dill sprigs, to garnish

FIRST MAKE THE STOCK. Rinse the fish bones in cold water. Roughly chop the vegetables then sauté them slowly in olive oil for 3–5 minutes so that they do not colour. Add the white wine, bay leaves, peppercorns and salt and boil for 5 minutes. Add the fish bones and the water. Bring back to the boil, reduce the heat and leave to simmer for 30 minutes. Pour the stock through a strainer, reserving the liquid and discarding the fish bones and vegetables.

TO MAKE THE SOUP, put the white wine in a large saucepan and let it simmer for 5 minutes. Add the reserved fish stock, the lemon juice, cream and saffron and bring slowly to the boil.

ADD THE LEEK, CARROT, CRAYFISH AND PRAWNS TO THE SOUP. Reduce the heat and let it simmer for 5 minutes. Meanwhile, cut the salmon and pollack into 2cm cubes. Add the cubed fish and let it simmer for 2 minutes more. Season to taste with salt and freshly ground pepper, then serve very hot garnished with dill.

PICNIC IN THE SNOW. When you go out for a whole day cross-country skiing in the mountains, you need to bring a solid lunch that will keep you energized and warm. Spinach soup (you can use frozen spinach if you cannot buy it fresh) and a smoked salmon and avocado sandwich is perfect. Pack the vacuum jug of soup in your basket or rucksack along with your sandwiches and some paper cups and spoons. Enjoy them together in the cold, white mountains.

Spinach soup *(Serves 4)*

1kg fresh spinach
2 tbsp olive oil
1 onion, roughly chopped
2 garlic cloves,
roughly chopped
2 large potatoes, peeled
and cubed
1 litre water
½ tsp freshly ground mace
salt and pepper
100ml double cream

TO MAKE THE SOUP, remove any tough stems from the spinach leaves and rinse them three or four times in cold water. Drain and set aside in a colander. Heat the olive oil in a large saucepan and sauté the onion and garlic. Stir in the potatoes and 500ml of the water. Bring to the boil, then reduce the heat and leave to simmer for 15 minutes.

ADD THE SPINACH, MACE, SALT, FRESHLY GROUND PEPPER and the rest of the water to the pan. Return to the boil, then reduce the heat, cover and leave to simmer for 10 minutes. Add the cream and heat through. Blend the soup (using a hand-held blender is the easiest way to do it) and adjust the salt and pepper to taste. Store the hot soup in a vacuum jug ready to take on the picnic.

Smoked salmon sandwich *(Serves 4)*

8 slices bread, 4 rolls or
4 pieces rye focaccia
(page 76), split horizontally
200g mixed salad leaves
12 slices smoked salmon
2 tomatoes, sliced
1 avocado, sliced

SANDWICH CREAM
3 tbsp mayonnaise
(page 92)
2 tbsp yoghurt
1 tsp Djion mustard
1 tsp grated organic
lemon zest
salt and pepper

COMBINE ALL THE INGREDIENTS FOR THE SANDWICH CREAM in a bowl and mix together, adding salt and freshly ground pepper to taste.

SPREAD THE CREAM ON HALF THE BREAD SLICES, or the bottoms of the rolls or focaccia pieces. Divide the salad leaves between each sandwich and layer with the smoked salmon, tomato and avocado. Top with the remaining slices of bread (or roll or focaccia tops), cut in half if desired, and wrap each sandwich in cling film, ready to be packed for the picnic.

Lumpfish roe, which is crisp and has a salty taste, like a salty winter sea, is eaten raw, rinsed only in cold water. Usually it is served with blinis or toast, but I love it with crisp potato cakes.

Potato cakes with lumpfish roe and beetroot salad *(Serves 6)*

BEETROOT SALAD

2 beetroot, about 500g each

juice of 1 lime

salt and pepper

POTATO CAKES

600g potatoes, peeled and shredded

4 spring onions, finely chopped

4 eggs

4 tbsp oatmeal

1 tbsp sesame seeds

1 tsp grated nutmeg

1 tbsp thyme leaves

2 tbsp olive oil

TO SERVE

2 tbsp finely chopped chives

150ml half-fat crème fraîche

400g lumpfish roe, rinsed

PREHEAT THE OVEN to 180°C (Gas 4). Put the beetroot on a baking tray and cook them in the oven for 30 minutes. Take them out and let them cool slightly before peeling them. Cut the beetroot into very small cubes and toss with the lime juice, salt and freshly ground pepper.

MEANWHILE, MAKE THE POTATO CAKES. In a mixing bowl, combine the shredded potatoes, spring onions, eggs, oatmeal, sesame seeds, nutmeg, thyme leaves and some salt and pepper.

HEAT THE OIL IN A FRYING PAN over a medium heat. Use a small spoon to form small cakes and place them in the oil, pressing down lightly so they are flat. Fry on each side for 5 minutes or until crisp. Meanwhile, stir the chopped chives into the crème fraîche.

PUT THE POTATO CAKES ON A SERVING DISH. Top with 1 tablespoon of the lumpfish roe, ½ tablespoon of the beetroot salad and some of the chive cream. Lastly, grind some pepper over the top and serve straight away with aquavit and beer.

When I was a little girl, I would often spend New Year's Eve with my grandfather on Ærø, an island in the south of Denmark. My aunt would be the hostess on New Year's Eve and cook the dinner. As always, it was cod with mustard sauce and all these lovely condiments. I loved that dinner: the whole atmosphere, the quietness, and the lovely light taste of the cod contrasting with the strong mustard sauce. Then, just after midnight, I would walk home with my grandfather in the new-fallen, squeaking snow. Some suppers can tell stories.

Cod with mustard sauce and condiments *(Serves 6–8)*

1 whole cod, rinsed
salt and pepper
1kg fingerling potatoes
8 organic eggs
200g bacon, diced
300g pickled beetroot
(page 148), diced

MUSTARD SAUCE
30g butter
2 tbsp plain wheat flour
400ml fish broth (from
cooking the cod)
4 tbsp wholegrain mustard
100ml double cream

PUT THE WHOLE COD IN A LARGE POT or fish kettle with some salt and freshly ground pepper. Add enough water to half cover the cod. Cover the pan with a lid and bring it to the boil, then reduce the heat and leave to simmer slowly for 20 minutes. Keep the fish warm in the pot with the lid on.

BOIL THE FINGERLING POTATOES IN A LARGE PAN of salted water until tender and keep them warm. Boil the eggs for 8–10 minutes, until hard, then peel them and cut each one in half. Fry the diced bacon until crisp.

NOW PREPARE THE SAUCE. Melt the butter in a small saucepan over a low heat, then add the flour and stir until it forms a smooth paste that comes away from the sides of the pan. Strain 400ml of the cooking liquid from the cod, then add gradually to the pan, stirring well after each addition so that no lumps form as the sauce thickens. Add the mustard and cream and stir again until the sauce is smooth and is just coming to the boil. Season to taste with salt and pepper and remove from the heat.

LIFT THE COD OUT OF THE POT and place on a serving dish ready to carve at the table. Put the potatoes, eggs, bacon, beetroot and mustard sauce in dishes ready for people to add to their plates as desired.

The quality of Scandinavian lamb is high. Our sheep live on hillsides, meadows or marshes – all places where the winter weather in particular can be rather rough, with high winds, rain and even snow. The lambs are exercised as they move around, following the low ebb and the high tide, and so their meat is very tender. This stew is especially nice when the weather is wet and chilly.

Lamb stew with rosemary mash *(Serves 6)*

2 tbsp olive oil

1kg lamb shoulder, cut into even-sized chunks

2 garlic cloves, chopped

2 rosemary sprigs

10 sage leaves

300ml white wine

200ml water

300g Jerusalem artichokes, peeled and cubed

2 leeks, thickly sliced

2 apples, cored and cubed

salt and pepper

MASH

1kg potatoes, peeled and cut into large cubes

2 garlic cloves

2 rosemary sprigs

1 tbsp whole peppercorns

1 tbsp coarse salt

50g butter

IN A SAUTÉ PAN, HEAT THE OIL AND COOK THE MEAT until lightly coloured. Add the garlic, rosemary and sage, then pour in the wine and water and leave the meat to simmer for 45 minutes.

MEANWHILE, MAKE THE MASH. Put the potatoes in a saucepan with the garlic, rosemary, peppercorns and salt. Add enough water to cover the potatoes, cover with a lid and bring to the boil. Reduce the heat and leave the potatoes to simmer for 20 minutes. Drain the water from the potatoes, reserving it in a bowl for later. Remove the rosemary stems.

RETURN THE POTATOES TO THE PAN AND ADD THE BUTTER. Use a balloon whisk to mash the potatoes, leaving the mixture lumpy. If the mash is too heavy, add 100–200ml of the reserved cooking water. Put the pan back over the heat for a couple of minutes and stir with a wooden spoon.

TO FINISH THE STEW, add the Jerusalem artichokes and simmer for 10 minutes, then add the leeks and apples and simmer for 5 minutes more. Season to taste with salt and freshly ground pepper and serve straight away with the mash.

A TREAT FOR COLD AFTERNOONS. If life were perfect, we would have more time to drink hot chocolate with our family and friends. One day, during a long and busy spell of hard work, I decided to arrive home early, bake buns and make hot chocolate for my children as a surprise. It was an especially nasty day outside: snowing, cold and windy. I got home, made everything ready, lit the candles and sat down, and waited … and waited. Nobody came home that afternoon. They were all busy with their lives on the very day I had decided to do something different with mine. The buns and cocoa were reheated later that night and still tasted wonderful.

Cardamom buns (Makes 28)

50g fresh yeast
750ml lukewarm milk
50g butter, melted and left to cool a little
1kg plain wheat flour
1 tsp ground cardamom
2 tbsp caster sugar
2 tsp salt
1 egg, beaten

DISSOLVE THE YEAST IN THE LUKEWARM MILK in a mixing bowl, then add the melted butter. Sift the flour, cardamom, sugar and salt together and stir the dry ingredients into the milk mixture. When a dough has formed that comes cleanly from the edges of the bowl, turn it out onto a floured work surface and knead for 5 minutes.

RETURN THE DOUGH TO THE BOWL, cover with a tea towel and leave to rise in a warm place for 1 hour. Tip the dough out onto the work surface and knead it again, then shape it into 28 small buns. Place them on two baking trays lined with baking paper. Cover with tea towels and leave to rise again for 20 minutes.

PREHEAT THE OVEN to 200°C (Gas 6). Lightly glaze each bun with beaten egg and bake for 20–25 minutes. Make the hot chocolate while the cardamom buns are in the oven. Serve the freshly baked buns with butter on the side.

Hot chocolate (Serves 4)

250g good-quality dark chocolate
1 litre whole milk
1 tsp caster sugar
200ml double cream

MELT THE CHOCOLATE VERY GENTLY in a small, heavy-based saucepan, then add a little bit of the milk and stir until smooth. Repeat until half of the milk is used, then add the sugar. Stir in the rest of the milk.

BRING THE HOT CHOCOLATE TO JUST UNDER BOILING POINT, stirring constantly so that it does not burn. Turn the heat off. Whip the cream until it forms soft peaks. (If you are not serving the hot chocolate immediately, keep the cream cold until you are ready to use it.)

SERVE THE HOT CHOCOLATE with spoonfuls of the cold whipped cream on top. Serve with freshly baked cardamom buns and butter.

March

This time of year is neither winter nor spring. In March you long for spring to arrive while the winter stubbornly refuses to retire. The gloominess of the month can be quite beautiful and puts you in a melancholy, reflective mood. Food is one of the best ways to comfort yourself. Mussels are perfect at this time, also soups and warm stews. Most importantly: a kartoffelkage will raise the spirits and make you appreciate any gloomy March day.

This is the best and cheapest dish ever. We have lots of mussels in the seas around Scandinavia – the blue ones are most common and there are plenty of them. They are easy to prepare and cost almost nothing, so they are the perfect thing to cook on a cold, romantic winter's night when you dream of early spring.

Limfjords mussels steamed in wine, vegetables and parsley *(Serves 2)*

1kg mussels
1 tbsp olive oil
2 garlic cloves, chopped
1 carrot, cut into thin strips
1 leek, cut into thin strips
200ml white wine
10 thyme sprigs
salt and pepper
200ml double cream
6 tbsp chopped flat-leaf parsley

SCRUB THE MUSSELS thoroughly and tug out any beards that may be hanging from the shells. Discard any broken or open mussels or those that refuse to close when the shells are tapped. Rinse the mussels in cold water a couple of times.

IN A LARGE SAUCEPAN, HEAT THE OIL and slowly cook the garlic for a couple of minutes. Add the mussels, vegetables, white wine, thyme, and some salt and freshly ground pepper. Stir gently then put the lid on and leave to simmer for 5 minutes.

ADD THE CREAM and parsley and simmer for 2 more minutes. Discard any mussels that have not opened. Season to taste with salt and pepper then eat straight away with a lovely loaf of bread and a nice bottle of wine.

Another tradition at this time of year is to eat fish roe. You can buy a lot of different roe products in Scandinavia. Sweden's supermarkets have a huge selection of paste products in tubes: they are very salty and you eat them on bread for breakfast and lunch. I prefer freshly boiled cod's roe sliced and served on a piece of rye bread with a creamy herb dressing.

Smørrebrød: cod's roe on rye bread *(Serves 4)*

500g cod's roe
1 tbsp sea salt
4 slices rye bread
butter, for spreading
dill sprigs, to garnish

DRESSING
2 tbsp crème fraîche
2 tbsp mayonnaise (page 92)
1 tbsp lemon juice
1 tbsp chopped dill
1 tbsp chopped chives
sea salt and pepper

PUT THE COD'S ROE IN A SAUCEPAN with a generous quantity of water and the sea salt. Boil for 30 minutes, then remove the roe with a draining spoon and leave to cool.

MEANWHILE, MAKE THE DRESSING. In a small bowl combine the crème fraîche, mayonnaise, lemon juice and herbs and season with salt and freshly ground pepper.

WHEN THE COD'S ROE HAS COOLED, CUT IT INTO SLICES. Spread the rye bread with butter and arrange them on four plates. Put four or five slices of cod's roe on each piece of rye bread. Top with a tablespoon of the herb dressing and garnish with dill. Serve for lunch with cold beer.

In March the sea is very cold and the lakes and rivers in the northern part of Scandinavia are frozen solid. Nevertheless, many people take a swim at this time of year – it is very healthy and some people believe that it prolongs life. Right after you come out of the cold water, you go into the sauna. Later on you deserve a nice bowl of tasty, hot soup – there is nothing like it on a cold winter's night.

Yoghurt and whole wheat bread *(Makes 2 loaves)*

200g whole wheat grains
500ml water, plus extra for glazing
400ml low-fat yoghurt
50g fresh yeast
3 tbsp vegetable oil
2 tsp salt
1 tsp caster sugar
400g wholegrain spelt flour
400g plain wheat flour, plus extra for dusting

PUT THE WHOLE WHEAT GRAINS IN A SAUCEPAN with the water and bring to the boil. Reduce the heat and leave to simmer, uncovered, for 15 minutes. Remove the pan from the heat, pour the contents into a mixing bowl and leave to cool a little.

MIX IN THE YOGHURT. Add the yeast and stir until it has dissolved, then stir in the oil, salt and sugar. Lastly add the two flours and keep stirring until the dough leaves the sides of the bowl.

TURN THE DOUGH OUT onto a floured work surface and knead for 10 minutes. Put the dough back in the bowl, cover with a tea towel and set aside to rise for 1 hour at room temperature.

AFTER IT HAS RISEN, DIVIDE THE DOUGH IN TWO, knead very lightly and shape into round loaves. Place each one on an oven tray lined with baking paper. Leave to rise again for 20 minutes.

PREHEAT THE OVEN to 200°C (Gas 6). Glaze the loaves with some extra water before they go into the oven. Bake for 45 minutes. The bread is done when you knock on the base of each loaf and it sounds hollow. Leave to cool on a wire rack.

Jerusalem artichoke soup *(Serves 4)*

1kg Jerusalem artichokes, cubed
1 leek, sliced
2 garlic cloves, chopped
2 tsp salt
1 litre water
1 beetroot
100ml single cream
salt and pepper
500ml vegetable oil

PUT THE JERUSALEM ARTICHOKES in a medium-sized saucepan with the leek, garlic, salt and water. Bring to the boil, then reduce the heat and leave to simmer for 15 minutes. Meanwhile, peel the beetroot, then use a potato peeler to cut it into long ribbons. Set them aside to drain on a paper towel.

WHIZZ THE SOUP IN A BLENDER or food processor until smooth, then return it to the saucepan. Add the cream and bring to the boil, stirring constantly. Season to taste with salt and freshly ground pepper and keep warm.

HEAT THE VEGETABLE OIL IN A SAUTÉ PAN and fry the beetroot ribbons for a few minutes. Remove them from the oil with a slotted spoon or spider and leave to drain on paper towels.

SERVE THE SOUP HOT, garnished with the beetroot.

There are many different kinds of oysters in Scandinavia. My favourites are from Limfjorden, a bay in northern Jutland. The shells are circular, and the oysters are big and very meaty. It is a shame to eat them anything but plain, but if you insist on some kind of sauce, serve them with this red onion vinaigrette.

Oysters (Serves 4)

24 Limfjords oysters
lemon wedges, to serve

WHISK THE RED WINE VINEGAR with the sugar until the sugar has dissolved. Mix the red onion into the vinegar and set aside.

VINAIGRETTE
4 tbsp red wine vinegar
2 tbsp caster sugar
1 small red onion, very finely chopped

OPEN THE OYSTERS WITH AN OYSTER KNIFE and release the meat from the bottom shell so that it is easy to eat at the table. Serve the oysters with the red onion vinaigrette and lemon wedges.

Captain's stew is made of potatoes and meat with bay leaves and lots of black pepper. This is one of my favourite winter dishes. I do not prepare it often, only a couple of times each winter. It's solid and tasty and will fill you up for quite some time.

Captain's stew (Serves 6)

4 tbsp olive oil
1kg chuck steak, cut into even-sized chunks
1.5 litres water
2kg potatoes, peeled and diced
1 onion, finely chopped
4 bay leaves
1 tbsp whole peppercorns
1 tbsp sea salt
50g butter
salt and pepper

TO SERVE
chopped chives
wholegrain mustard
sliced rye bread
pickled beetroot (page 148)

HEAT THE OIL IN A LARGE SAUCEPAN and, when medium-hot, add the chuck steak and fry the meat until lightly coloured. Add the water and bring gradually to the boil, skimming any froth from the surface (it takes about 5 minutes to catch it all).

ADD THE POTATOES, ONION, BAY LEAVES, PEPPERCORNS AND SALT. Simmer for 1½ hours, or until the meat is very tender and falls apart easily – you may need to cook it for another 30 minutes or so.

STIR IN THE BUTTER. Use a balloon whisk to mash the potatoes and meat together – though note that the stew has to remain lumpy. Season with salt and freshly ground pepper.

SERVE SPRINKLED WITH THE CHOPPED CHIVES and accompanied by wholegrain mustard, slices of rye bread and pickled beetroot.

This dish is best as a Sunday lunch, or as a hangover cure after a long night out. This is my Swedish version, but there are many variations. In Denmark, bøf tartar is a dish of raw meat with all the condiments and an egg yolk served on top. I'm not a fan of raw meat (I like raw fish better) and therefore prefer biff Lindström to bøf tartar.

Biff Lindström *(Serves 4)*

1 onion, finely chopped
2 tbsp capers, finely chopped
2 tbsp pickled beetroot (page 148), finely chopped
2 tbsp finely chopped chives
500g minced beef
4 egg yolks
1 tbsp Worcestershire sauce
salt and pepper
olive oil, for frying

FRIED POTATOES
1kg potatoes
40g butter
2 tbsp olive oil

BALSAMICO BEANS
300g green beans
3 tbsp balsamic vinegar
2 tsp caster sugar

COMBINE THE ONION, CAPERS, BEETROOT AND CHIVES in a mixing bowl with the minced beef, egg yolks, Worcestershire sauce, salt and freshly ground pepper. Shape the mixture into four hamburgers and season on both sides with salt and pepper.

BOIL THE POTATOES IN A LARGE PAN of salted water until tender, then drain. Once they are cool enough to handle, peel them and cut the flesh into even-sized cubes. Heat the butter and olive oil in a sauté pan and fry the potatoes for about 10 minutes, turning them regularly. Sprinkle with salt and pepper.

STEAM THE BEANS for 5 minutes and drain them well. In a small saucepan, stir together the balsamic vinegar and sugar and leave to simmer for 3 minutes. Toss the beans in the balsamico glaze until hot.

MEANWHILE, FRY THE BURGERS in olive oil for 3–8 minutes on each side, depending on whether you want them medium or well-done. Serve with the potatoes and balsamico beans on the side.

You can buy this traditional cake, which looks like a large potato (kartoffel), in most bakeries around Denmark. Choux pastry is covered with cocoa-dusted marzipan and filled with the most luscious cream you can imagine. If you like to bake, then take the time one day to prepare this pastry. I promise: you are not going to regret it.

Kartoffelkage (Makes 8)

CHOUX PASTRY
80g butter, plus extra for greasing
200ml water
pinch of salt
100g plain wheat flour
2–3 eggs, beaten

CREAM
1 vanilla pod
250ml single cream
3 egg yolks
3 tbsp caster sugar
1 tbsp cornflour
100ml double cream

MARZIPAN TOPPING
400g ready-rolled marzipan
100g cocoa powder

TO MAKE THE PASTRY, put the butter and water in a saucepan over a low heat and allow the butter to melt. Now turn up the heat and bring the mixture to the boil.

SIFT THE SALT INTO THE FLOUR. Turn off the heat under the pan, add the flour to the liquid and stir with a wooden spoon until a firm, smooth paste is formed. Beat the paste until it comes away from the edges of the pot in a ball. Leave to cool for about 10 minutes. Add the beaten eggs little by little, beating well each time. Continue adding egg until the mixture is smooth and glossy. Sometimes you need to use all the beaten eggs, sometimes not, so it is fine if a little is left over.

PUT THE DOUGH IN A PIPING BAG with a 0.5cm plain nozzle. Lightly grease a sheet of baking paper and place on a baking tray. To one side of the paper, pipe a 6cm line of choux pastry. Follow with a second line parallel to the first one, so that they cling together. Pipe a third line on top of the other two. Repeat to give eight of these choux buns.

PREHEAT THE OVEN to 200°C (Gas 6), then bake the buns for 20–30 minutes. Do not open the oven door before the choux has set or the pastry may not rise. The pastries are done when they are golden brown and firm. Place them on a wire rack. Cut a small hole in the side of each bun to let the steam out, so the pastry will not go soft inside. Leave to cool.

CUT THE VANILLA POD IN HALF LENGTHWAYS and scrape out the seeds with the tip of a knife. Put the vanilla seeds with the single cream in a saucepan and heat until steaming hot. Meanwhile, whisk the egg yolks and sugar together in a mixing bowl until the mixture turns pale and fluffy, then whisk in the cornflour. Stir one-third of the hot cream into the egg mixture, then pour the egg mixture into the saucepan. Stir over a low heat until it starts to thicken. Remove from the heat and leave to cool. When the cream filling is cold, whip the double cream until it forms stiff peaks and fold it in.

SPLIT EACH CHOUX BUN IN HALF HORIZONTALLY and place a couple of spoonfuls of cream filling on the bottom half. Place the other half on top, being careful not to press them together. Take the marzipan and cut it into eight oval shapes about 8cm long, using an oval pastry cutter or a small, sharp knife. Lay the marzipan ovals on a piece of baking paper and dust them with cocoa powder until they are completely covered. Carefully lay one over each cream-filled pastry.

PLACE THE FILLED PASTRIES ON A SERVING DISH and keep cool until serving time. I prefer them served with good coffee or espresso – the bitterness of the coffee goes well the luscious gateau.

April

Copenhagen bursts into life in early spring. Everybody comes out of their houses or flats, the cafés put tables and chairs on the pavement, all the small beautiful squares become populated again, and there are lots of cultural events and festivals. It's a great time to sit outside, lunching on herrings and drinking the famous beer and aquavit.

Herrings live in the chill waters that surround the Scandinavian coast. Some people have them for lunch daily; they are an important part of meals at special occasions such as Easter, too. Serve three or four different kinds of herrings at one meal and eat them on rye bread with sliced raw onion and dill on top.

Marinated fried herrings *(Serves 4)*

BRINE

500ml spirit vinegar
300g caster sugar
1 tbsp whole peppercorns
4 bay leaves

HERRING

12 fresh herring fillets
4 tbsp Dijon mustard
1 bunch dill, chopped
200g rye flour
75g butter
2 onions, sliced

COMBINE ALL THE INGREDIENTS for the brine in a saucepan and bring to the boil, then reduce the heat and leave to simmer for 30 minutes. Remove from the heat and set aside to cool.

TO PREPARE THE HERRING, cut off the little fin on the back side of each fillet. In a small bowl, mix the Dijon mustard and dill together. Spread out the rye flour on a tray or large plate.

PLACE THE HERRING FILLETS SKIN-SIDE DOWN in the flour, pressing them down a bit so that the flour sticks to them. Spread 1 teaspoon of the mustard mixture over each herring and fold them over so that the fillets form a square sandwich. Make sure the skin is covered in rye flour.

HEAT THE BUTTER in a frying pan and cook the herring for 3–5 minutes on each side, depending on size.

PLACE THE COOKED HERRINGS in a large plastic box, laying them side by side. Scatter the sliced onions over the herrings, then cover with the brine and leave to marinate for 2 hours, or overnight in the refrigerator. They will keep for up to a week in the refrigerator.

Homemade white herrings *(Serves 12)*

12 salted herring fillets
1 red onion, sliced
2 carrots, thinly sliced
2 dill sprigs, fronds picked off

BRINE

400ml water
250ml caster sugar
2 bay leaves
2 tbsp whole peppercorns
1 tbsp coriander seeds
2 tbsp mustard seeds
10 whole cloves
400ml vinegar
15 allspice

COVER THE SALTED HERRING FILLETS with cold water and leave them to soak for 6 hours.

COMBINE ALL THE INGREDIENTS for the brine in a saucepan and bring to the boil, then reduce the heat and leave to simmer for 30 minutes. Remove from the heat and set aside to cool.

DRAIN THE HERRING FILLETS and cut them into 3cm slices. Place them in a sterilized preserving jar with the sliced onion, carrots and dill fronds. Pour over the cold brine, seal tightly and leave in the refrigerator for a week before eating. Then simply fish out the pieces of herring and any parts of the brine as desired. Stored in the refrigerator, the herrings will last for up to 3 months.

Smoked salmon used to be something special that you would eat only at dinner parties or on special occasions, but this has changed as prices have come down. If you buy a whole side of smoked salmon, you can cut it into three or four pieces and freeze them separately. Freshly cut smoked salmon tastes far better than pre-cut slices, so try to do it yourself.

Smoked salmon and horseradish cream with crunchy cucumber and caraway seed salad *(Serves 4)*

300g mixed green salad leaves
1 cucumber
1 tbsp caraway seeds
12 slices smoked salmon

DRESSING
300ml half-fat crème fraîche
½ tsp sugar
2 tbsp grated fresh horseradish,
or preserved horseradish
1 tbsp lemon juice
salt and pepper

TEAR THE SALAD LEAVES into smaller pieces. Cut the cucumber in half lengthways and then cut it into thin slices. Mix the salad leaves, cucumber and caraway seeds in a salad bowl.

TO MAKE THE DRESSING, mix the crème fraîche, sugar and horseradish together, stirring very gently, because if you beat half-fat crème fraîche it becomes runny. Add the lemon juice and season with salt and freshly ground pepper.

TOSS HALF THE DRESSING INTO THE SALAD and put the rest into a dish to hand around separately. Arrange the smoked salmon on plates with the dressed salad on the side. Serve with nice home-baked bread, such as caraway seed bread or yogurt and whole wheat loaf (see pages 92 and 48).

Smørrebrød (sometimes called 'open sandwiches') are traditionally served at lunchtime, though I also like to eat them for supper on Sunday. This is the perfect meal to serve guests staying for the weekend, in which case I prepare them with different toppings such as those on pages 14, 44 and 118. If you can't find lovage, use tarragon or parsley.

Smørrebrød: chicken and lovage salad on rye bread *(Serves 4)*

1 bunch lovage
1 small chicken
1 tbsp sea salt
1 tbsp whole peppercorns
2 tbsp half-fat crème fraîche
2 tbsp mayonnaise (page 92)
salt and pepper

TO SERVE
4 slices rye bread
crunchy lettuce leaves

PICK THE LEAVES from four stems of the lovage and set them aside for the salad. Put the chicken in a pot with the four lovage stems, salt and peppercorns. Add enough water to cover the chicken. Bring to the boil, then reduce the heat and leave to simmer for 1 hour.

WHEN THE CHICKEN IS COOKED, carefully lift it out of the water and place on a tray. Once it is cool enough to handle, remove the skin and peel the chicken meat off the bones, discarding the bones and skin.

CHOP THE RESERVED LOVAGE LEAVES. Put the chicken pieces in a mixing bowl with 6 tablespoons of the chopped lovage, plus the crème fraîche and mayonnaise. Fold together and season to taste with salt and freshly ground pepper.

ARRANGE THE SLICES OF RYE BREAD ON FOUR PLATES, then place the lettuce on the bread and add the chicken salad. Take the remaining lovage stems and cut them in two lengthways. Use them to garnish the smørrebrød before serving.

Combining different vegetables in all kinds of salads has always been one of the things I love most about cooking. I started preparing salads when I was a child. I was in charge of the cooking once every week. I took everything out of the fridge and, without knowing the rules, combined them. Some days it was fantastic – other days did not go so well. But I learned a lot, and one of the most important lessons was: to taste.

Baked green and white asparagus salad *(Serves 4)*

15 green asparagus spears
15 white asparagus spears
4 tbsp extra virgin olive oil
grated zest and juice of
1 organic lemon
salt and pepper

PREHEAT THE OVEN to 180°C (Gas 4). Cut 3cm from the base of each asparagus spear, then peel the white ones only from the head down. Rinse the asparagus with the tips downwards in cold water. Place the spears in an ovenproof dish and mix well with the olive oil, lemon zest and juice and some salt and freshly ground pepper.

BAKE THE SPEARS for 5–7 minutes. You can then serve them as they are, hot or cold, or cut the spears into smaller pieces, making sure the lemon zest and juice are still coating the asparagus.

Cauliflower with coarse almonds *(Serves 4)*

1 medium-sized cauliflower
75g whole almonds
1 garlic clove, crushed
juice of 1 lemon
1 tbsp white wine vinegar
4 tbsp olive oil
4 tbsp chopped chervil or
flat-leafed parsley
salt and pepper

RINSE AND DRY THE CAULIFLOWER, cut it into very small florets and place in a bowl.

CHOP THE ALMONDS UNTIL MEDIUM-FINE and mix them together with the crushed garlic, lemon juice, vinegar and olive oil, plus some salt and pepper.

MIX THE DRESSING WITH THE CAULIFLOWER and leave to rest for 30 minutes. Season the salad to taste with salt and freshly ground pepper, then sprinkle with chervil or parsley before serving.

Carrot salad with parsley and pine nuts *(Serves 4)*

4 carrots
2 tbsp pine nuts
30g flat-leafed parsley,
roughly chopped
2 tbsp olive oil
juice of 1 lemon
salt and pepper

PEEL THE CARROTS and trim off the bottoms and tops. Use the peeler to cut the carrots into ribbons.

IN A DRY FRYING PAN, TOAST THE PINE NUTS, stirring constantly until they are golden brown.

IN A SALAD BOWL, COMBINE the carrots, pine nuts, parsley, olive oil and lemon juice. Season to taste with salt and freshly ground pepper before serving.

Meatballs are a national favourite in many countries and served in many different ways. I grow lots of thyme in my small urban garden from May until September, so that I have it right at hand. Instead of boiling cabbage to serve with the meatballs, I prefer to fry it in butter so that it stays crisp and retains its nutty taste. Cowberries grow in cold areas and are very sour, like cranberries. You therefore need to cook them with a lot of sugar, but I still like to keep the taste quite fresh and sour.

Meatballs with thyme, summer cabbage and lingonsylt *(Serves 4)*

700g mixture of minced veal and pork
1 small onion, finely chopped
3 tbsp thyme leaves, finely chopped
2 eggs
75g fresh breadcrumbs
2 tbsp plain wheat flour
100ml sparkling water
salt and pepper
700g new baby potatoes
olive oil
about 40g butter
1 pointed cabbage, quartered lengthways
cowberry compote (below)

TO MAKE THE MEATBALLS, mix the minced meats, onion, thyme and eggs together and beat well. Stir in the breadcrumbs and flour and beat again. Lastly mix in the sparkling water and season with salt and freshly ground pepper.

PREHEAT THE OVEN to 180°C (Gas 4). Cut the potatoes in half lengthways. Put them an ovenproof dish and mix them with a little olive oil, salt and pepper. Bake the potatoes for 1 hour.

MEANWHILE, USE A SPOON AND YOUR FREE HAND TO SHAPE THE MEAT MIXTURE into small round balls. Heat 10g of the butter and some olive oil together in a large frying pan and cook the meatballs on all sides until they are golden brown. Transfer the meatballs to an ovenproof dish and put them in the oven for 10 minutes to finish cooking.

ONCE THE MEATBALLS ARE IN THE OVEN, melt the remaining butter in a large frying pan and fry the cabbage in it for a couple of minutes on each side of the wedge. Sprinkle with pepper and serve the cabbage together with the meatballs, potatoes and cowberry compote.

Cowberry compote

1kg fresh or frozen lingon (cowberries) or cranberries
200ml water
600g caster sugar

COMBINE THE FRUIT AND WATER IN A SAUCEPAN and bring to the boil. Reduce the heat and simmer for about 8 minutes, skimming the froth from the surface.

ADD THE SUGAR AND STIR TO DISSOLVE then boil the mixture for 8 minutes. Pour the hot compote into a large sterilized preserving jar (or some small jars). As soon as it is cold it is ready to eat, but stored in the refrigerator it will last for up to 3 months.

I love cucumber salad. The sweet and sour flavour takes me back to my childhood holidays at the beach, staying with my grandparents. My grandmother would serve cucumber salad almost every day during spring and summer. She would reuse the dressing and just add freshly cut cucumber. This combination of dishes is also perfect served as a buffet for a party.

Veal with baked rhubarb, sweet and sour cucumber salad, and barley salad *(Serves 4)*

CUCUMBER SALAD

300ml spirit or malt vinegar

75g caster sugar

1 cucumber, cut into paper-thin slices

VEAL

1 veal rump, about 800g

salt and pepper

BAKED RHUBARB

5 spring rhubarb stalks, trimmed and cut into 5cm pieces

2 tbsp caster sugar

BARLEY SALAD

300g pearl barley

600ml water

1 tsp salt

1 red onion, finely chopped

30g flat-leafed parsley, finely chopped

100g raisins, roughly chopped

START THE CUCUMBER SALAD by combining the vinegar and sugar in a saucepan. Bring to the boil, then reduce the heat and leave to simmer for 5 minutes, stirring the mixture to make sure all the sugar dissolves. Set aside to cool.

PREHEAT THE OVEN to 200°C (Gas 6). Meanwhile, score the fat on top of the veal rump into a diamond pattern and rub thoroughly with salt and freshly ground pepper. Roast in the oven for 30 minutes.

BOIL THE BARLEY IN SALTED WATER for 20 minutes, then cover, turn off the heat and leave to rest in the hot water for 10 minutes.

FOLD THE RHUBARB PIECES GENTLY INTO THE SUGAR so they are just about coated. Place in an ovenproof dish and set aside.

DRAIN THE BARLEY THOROUGHLY, put in a large bowl and – while still hot – add the onion. Mix well and leave to cool, then add the parsley and raisins and season to taste with salt and pepper.

PLACE THE CUCUMBER SLICES IN A BOWL. Pour over the vinegar-sugar mixture, mix well and place in the refrigerator until ready to serve.

WHEN THE MEAT IS DONE, remove from the oven and leave it to rest for 10 minutes. Meanwhile, reduce the oven temperature to 175°C (Gas 4) and bake the rhubarb for 10 minutes.

CARVE THE VEAL INTO SLICES and serve with the baked rhubarb, cucumber salad and barley salad.

At the beginning of spring, rhubarb is pink and gives pink-coloured cordial, but as the season progresses, the darker rhubarb produces red cordial. It tastes wonderful diluted with still water, sparkling water or Champagne. The pudding below is to die for, and you can serve it all year round, just by switching the rhubarb for berries or other fruit. In summer, I prepare it with strawberries and raspberries, in autumn with apples and during winter with dried prunes and figs.

Rhubarb cordial *(Makes 1.5 litres)*

2kg rhubarb, trimmed and cut into 5cm pieces
800ml water
700g caster sugar

RINSE THE RHUBARB IN COLD WATER and drain well. Combine the rhubarb and water in a saucepan and bring to the boil, then reduce the heat and simmer for 30 minutes.

LINE A SIEVE WITH MUSLIN AND STRAIN THE COOKED RHUBARB THROUGH IT. Put the resulting rhubarb juice into a clean saucepan and bring to the boil with the sugar, stirring so that the sugar dissolves. Skim any froth from the surface and leave to simmer for 10 minutes.

POUR THE HOT LIQUID INTO STERILIZED BOTTLES and seal. When the cordial has cooled, store it in the refrigerator. To serve, mix one part rhubarb cordial with two parts cold water and serve over ice.

Rhubarb trifle *(Serves 6)*

MACAROONS
2 egg whites
100g caster sugar
100g whole almonds

TO MAKE THE MACAROONS, whisk the egg whites until they form stiff peaks. Add the sugar – just 2 tablespoons at a time – beating well after each addition. Whizz the almonds in a food processor until they are very finely ground, then fold them into the meringue mixture.

RHUBARB
500g rhubarb, trimmed and cut into 2cm pieces
100g caster sugar

PREHEAT THE OVEN to 180°C (Gas 4). Line a baking tray with baking paper and use a teaspoon to spoon about 25 small pyramids of the almond mixture onto it, keeping them a few centimetres apart. Bake for about 15 minutes or until golden brown. Carefully lift the baking paper from the tray with the macaroons still on it and transfer to a wire rack to cool. (You can do this a few days in advance and store the macaroons in an airtight tin.) Reduce the oven temperature to 150°C (Gas 2) ready to cook the rhubarb.

CREAM
1 vanilla pod
2 egg yolks
2 tbsp caster sugar
300ml double cream

RINSE THE RHUBARB IN COLD WATER and drain well. Place in an ovenproof dish, stir in the sugar and bake for 15 minutes. Remove from the oven and leave to cool.

CUT THE VANILLA POD IN HALF LENGTHWAYS and scrape out the seeds with the tip of a knife. Put the seeds in a bowl with the egg yolks and sugar and beat until pale and fluffy. In a separate bowl, whip the double cream until it forms soft peaks and fold it into the egg mixture. Place the cream mixture in the refrigerator to chill.

BREAK THE MACAROONS INTO SMALL CHUNKS. Now everything is ready to finish the trifle. You can either do it immediately so that the layers become soft and melded, or wait until just before serving so that the trifle is fresh and crunchy. Take four serving glasses and put a layer of cream at the bottom. Add the rhubarb, then the macaroons, and repeat the layers so that there are two of each ingredient. Now indulge. It is fantastic.

June

In June, we celebrate midsummer night, the longest evening of the year. It does not get dark at all on summer nights in the northernmost areas of Scandinavia, while in other parts it will stay light until around 12 o'clock. Summer begins in June and is a busy month for cooks, with lots of wonderful things to do. We usually get the first strawberries and new potatoes around midsummer. However, elderflowers have to be gathered as soon as they blossom because the season is short.

These tiny shrimps live in bay areas around Denmark and are caught during the summer. They are quite rare and therefore very expensive. You need to peel them, which is hard work. Bay shrimps have a very delicate taste and so should be eaten as freshly and simply as possible. I like them with caraway seed bread. Caraway is a common spice in Scandinavian kitchens and also used in aquavit and cheese. This traditional loaf tastes best the same day it is baked.

Bay shrimps with homemade mayonnaise (Serves 4)

400g bay shrimps
butter
caraway seed bread (below)
soft green salad leaves
4 slices lemon
dill sprigs, to garnish

MAYONNAISE
2 egg yolks
1 tsp Dijon mustard
2 tbsp lemon juice or vinegar
1 small garlic clove, crushed
salt and pepper
300ml extra virgin olive oil

PEEL THE SHRIMPS, or let your guests peel their own at the table. It takes time but it's fun and you can have a nicely chilled bottle of Alsace wine at the same time.

TO MAKE THE MAYONNAISE, put the eggs yolks in a small blender. Add the mustard, lemon juice (or vinegar), garlic and some salt and freshly ground pepper and blend for 5 minutes. Slowly add the olive oil drop by drop, blending until the mixture starts to thicken. Do not add the oil too quickly. Continue until the mayonnaise is thick and smooth, then adjust the seasoning to taste.

SPREAD THE BUTTER ON THE CARAWAY SEED BREAD. Cover with the lettuce, then the shrimps. Top with the mayo and garnish with a slice of lemon and some dill.

Caraway seed bread (Makes 1 loaf)

100ml lukewarm water
25g fresh yeast
250ml buttermilk
500g plain wheat flour, plus extra for dusting
1 tsp salt
1 tsp caster sugar
1 tbsp caraway seeds

GLAZE
1 egg, beaten
1 tbsp caraway seeds

PUT THE WATER IN A MIXING BOWL, add the yeast and stir to dissolve. Add the buttermilk and stir again. In another bowl, sift together the flour, salt, sugar and caraway seeds. Stir the dry ingredients into the yeast mixture, working the dough until it comes away cleanly from the edge of the bowl.

DUST A WORK SURFACE WITH FLOUR and knead the dough for about 5 minutes. Return the dough to the bowl, cover with a tea towel and set aside to rise for 1 hour at room temperature.

SHAPE THE RISEN DOUGH INTO A LOAF and place on a baking tray lined with baking paper. Leave the bread to rise again for 20 minutes. Preheat the oven to 200°C (Gas 6). Brush the bread with the beaten egg and sprinkle with caraway seeds, then bake for 40 minutes, or until the bread sounds hollow when you knock on its base.

LEAVE THE BREAD TO COOL ON A WIRE RACK. It tastes best when freshly baked or, alternatively, if toasted the next day.

MIDSUMMER NIGHT. Midsummer night is celebrated in Sweden on 22 June. It is a national holiday and the Swedes dance around the Maypole (majstang). In Denmark, midsummer night is more informal. On the evening of 23 June, friends and family come together for a nice meal, preferably at the beach. Afterwards, everyone goes to see the bonfires and the witch being sent off on her broom to Bloksbjerg. This is a perfect meal to share with friends on such a night. Pile the langoustine up on serving dishes and pass them around. Let everybody tuck in, have a good time, and enjoy the informal atmosphere, good wine and lovely company.

Langoustines with herb mayonnaise *(Serves 8)*

40 raw langoustines
2 lemons, sliced

HERB MAYONNAISE
4 egg yolks
30g chervil, chopped
2 tbsp chopped flat-leafed parsley
1 tsp Dijon mustard
2 tbsp lemon juice
1 garlic clove, crushed
600ml extra virgin olive oil
salt and pepper

TO MAKE THE HERB MAYONNAISE, put the eggs yolks in a small blender. Add the herbs, mustard, lemon juice, garlic and some salt and freshly ground pepper and blend for 5 minutes. Slowly add the olive oil, drop by drop, blending until the mixture starts to thicken. Do not add the oil too quickly. Continue until the mayonnaise is thick and smooth, then adjust the seasoning to taste.

COOK THE LANGOUSTINES UNDER A MEDIUM-HOT GRILL OR ON A BARBECUE for about 10 minutes, turning them two or three times. Serve them immediately with the herb mayonnaise, garnished with the freshly sliced lemon.

IF YOU WANT TO SERVE THE LANGOUSTINES AS A MAIN COURSE, double the quantity of shellfish and serve with the mayonnaise, a nice loaf of bread and a fresh, crisp salad.

Lamb can be eaten all year round, but for me it is a tradition to serve it on midsummer night with new potatoes and a summer cabbage salad with fresh peas – all the best ingredients of the season. You can ask your butcher to bone the leg of lamb for you.

Grilled leg of lamb with garlic and tarragon *(Serves 8)*

1 boned leg of lamb
salt and pepper
10 tarragon sprigs
6 garlic cloves

PREPARE A KETTLE BARBECUE ready for cooking.

LAY OUT THE LEG OF LAMB ON THE WORK SURFACE. Sprinkle with salt and freshly ground pepper, then cover with the tarragon and garlic. Fold up the meat and tie it at regular intervals with a piece of kitchen string to help it keep its shape.

LAY THE MEAT ON THE BARBECUE GRILL and cover with the lid. Cook for about 2 hours at medium heat, taking care that the leg of lamb does not burn underneath.

WHEN THE LAMB IS DONE, LET IT REST ON A BOARD for 10 minutes before carving. Serve with the salads on page 102.

Elderflower has the taste of summer freshness. It is a bit like the feeling you get when the sun is shining on an early morning in the countryside and a gentle breeze is blowing. When beautiful elderflowers bloom, you know that summer is here and it is time to prepare elderflower cordial.

Elderflower cordial *(Makes 2 litres)*

40 elderflower clusters
3 organic lemons, sliced
60g citric acid
2kg caster sugar
2 litres water

PUT THE ELDERFLOWERS, LEMONS AND CITRIC ACID IN A VERY LARGE HEATPROOF BOWL. Combine the sugar and water in a saucepan and bring to the boil, stirring until the sugar has dissolved. Pour the syrup over the elderflowers, cover with a tea towel and leave to rest for 3–5 days.

STRAIN THE MIXTURE, DISCARDING ALL THE SOLIDS. Pour any cordial that you are not going to use immediately into sterilized bottles and store them in a cool, dark place. To use the cordial, dilute to taste with still or sparkling water, or Champagne and serve with slices of lemon.

SUMMER SALADS. Fresh, crunchy cabbage makes a delightful salad in early summer and the recipe below pairs it with some of the best ingredients of the season. New potatoes are a real treat in Scandinavia, too. They are tiny and have a fresh, light taste. Once cooked, which doesn't take long, they stay firm and the skin comes off very easily. They taste fantastic served with cold butter and salt on a piece of rye bread – very easy and very delicious.

Pointed cabbage with dill and peas *(Serves 8)*

2 pointed cabbages, cut into long strips
100g almonds (optional)
100g bunch dill
500g fresh shelled peas

DRESSING
juice of 1 lemon
1 tbsp runny honey
100ml vegetable oil
salt and pepper

RINSE THE CABBAGE STRIPS THOROUGHLY then set aside to drain. If using the almonds, roast them in a moderate oven for about 10 minutes or until the almonds are lightly browned. Leave them to cool, then chop them.

CHOP OFF THE TOPS OF THE BUNCH OF DILL TO USE IN THE SALAD; keep the rest for another recipe. Combine the cabbage, almonds, peas and dill tops in a large salad bowl and toss.

TO MAKE THE DRESSING, stir together the lemon juice and honey, then slowly add the oil. Season to taste with salt and freshly ground pepper. Toss the salad with the dressing just before serving.

Potato salad with fresh herbs and spring onions *(Serves 8)*

2kg baby new potatoes, halved
50ml white wine vinegar
5 spring onions, cut into 5mm pieces
100g flat-leafed parsley, chopped
100g chervil, chopped
100g chives, finely chopped
2 tbsp finely chopped mint
50ml olive oil
salt and pepper

BOIL THE POTATOES IN A LARGE PAN of salted water until soft but still firm, then drain and put in a large bowl.

ADD THE WHITE WINE VINEGAR AND SPRING ONIONS to the bowl, mix gently and leave to cool.

JUST BEFORE SERVING, add the herbs, olive oil, and salt and freshly ground pepper to taste.

Strawberries are divine. We have many varieties that grow very well in our climate. They are, in general, small with a very sweet flavour. Once picked, they do not last long and therefore have to be eaten right away. Their season is very short too. It starts around midsummer and lasts for about 3 or 4 weeks. It is best to serve them cold with sugar and cream.

Strawberries and cream *(Serves 8)*

3kg small, sweet
strawberries, hulled
4 tbsp caster sugar
800ml ice-cold double cream

RINSE AND DRY THE STRAWBERRIES. Serve in a large bowl with sugar and cream on the side, letting your guests help themselves.

Meringues with strawberry-mint salsa *(Makes 10)*

MERINGUE
4 egg whites
200g caster sugar
1 tsp vinegar
a little vegetable oil,
for greasing

STRAWBERRY-MINT SALSA
500g strawberries, hulled
and cubed
10 mint leaves, finely
chopped
100ml elderflower cordial
(page 100)
200ml double cream

TO MAKE THE MERINGUE MIXTURE, put the egg whites in a large clean bowl and whisk with an electric mixer until they form stiff peaks. Add the sugar one spoonful at a time, whisking after each addition. (This takes time. For the perfect result, whisk for about 10 minutes or until the sugar completely dissolves and the meringue is glossy.) Finally, add the vinegar and whisk again.

LAY A PIECE OF NON-STICK BAKING PARCHMENT on a baking tray and brush it lightly with oil. Fit a piping bag with a 0.5cm plain nozzle and fill it with the meringue mixture. Pipe out ten round birds nests, 7cm in diameter, on the baking paper, keeping them well spaced.

PREHEAT THE OVEN to 150°C (Gas 2) and bake the meringues for 5 minutes at this temperature before reducing the heat to 130°C (Gas ½) and continuing to bake for another 20 minutes. Leave the meringues to cool on a wire rack.

PUT THE STRAWBERRIES AND MINT IN A BOWL and pour over the elderflower cordial. Mix together gently and set aside. Whip the cream until it forms soft peaks.

PLACE A MERINGUE ON EACH PLATE, add the whipped cream and top with the strawberry-mint salsa. Serve the meringues immediately.

This soft, bread-like cake originates in Funen, Denmark. I think it deserves to become world famous. Sweet and tender and best the same day it is baked, it is traditionally eaten in the morning or with the afternoon coffee, but I also think it is perfect with a cup of tea. The only problem with this cake is that I can eat almost half of it all by myself.

Brunsviger *(Serves 10)*

250ml lukewarm whole milk
50g fresh yeast
2 eggs
75g butter, melted
500g plain wheat flour
2 tbsp caster sugar
a pinch of salt

GLAZE
150g dark brown sugar
100g butter

POUR THE MILK INTO A BOWL, add the yeast and stir with a wooden spoon until the yeast has dissolved. Add the eggs and mix well, then add the melted butter.

SIFT THE FLOUR WITH THE SUGAR AND SALT then stir the dry ingredients into the yeast mixture to make a dough. When the dough comes cleanly from the edge of the bowl, transfer it to a floured work surface and knead for about 5 minutes. Return the dough to the bowl and leave to rise at room temperature for 30 minutes.

LINE A 40 x 50CM OVENPROOF DISH WITH BAKING PAPER and press the dough evenly out in the dish. Cover with a tea towel and leave to rise again for 15 minutes.

PREHEAT THE OVEN to 200°C (Gas 6). To make the glaze, melt the brown sugar and butter together in a saucepan, stirring until the mixture is smooth and the sugar is no longer crunchy. Do not let it boil.

PRESS YOUR FINGERS DOWN INTO THE RISEN DOUGH, making small indentations across the surface. Spread the glaze evenly over the dough, leaving a 1cm border. Bake for 25–30 minutes, then leave the brunsviger to cool a little before cutting it into pieces and serving.

July

The Scandinavian countryside can be many different things, from romantic and bountiful to austere and rugged. There are lakes, mountains and kilometre after kilometre of forest. The habitat is diverse for such a small area of the world, and with Scandinavia's very long coastline, you are usually not far from the sea. At the height of summer, roses bloom and all the summer vegetables are readily available. In July we have raspberries, redcurrants and cherries too.

BREAKFAST. Breakfast is an important meal in the northern part of the world. You cannot just eat a croissant and have a coffee on your way to work. We have a long tradition of heavy meals in the morning, although nowadays breakfast is becoming lighter. The perfect summer breakfast is yoghurt with rysteribs – that is, with shaken redcurrants: fresh, sweet and very healthy because the fruit has a high level of vitamin C.

Yogurt with shaken redcurrants and rye bread topping *(Serves 8–10)*

SHAKEN REDCURRANTS
300g redcurrants, destalked
200g caster sugar

RYE BREAD SPRINKLE
100g dry rye bread
2 tbsp dark brown sugar

TO SERVE
low-fat yogurt

TO MAKE THE SHAKEN REDCURRANTS, rinse the redcurrants in cold water and drain them well. Spread them out on a large tray and sprinkle with the sugar. Shake the tray and then leave until the sugar has dissolved (it takes a couple of hours), shaking the tray occasionally.

WHEN THE SUGAR HAS DISSOLVED, pour the mixture into a sterilized preserving jar, seal tightly and store in the refrigerator for up to 3 weeks.

TO MAKE THE RYE BREAD SPRINKLE, use your fingers to break the rye bread into small pieces. Spread them out on a baking tray and toast in the oven for 15 minutes at 100°C (Gas ¼). Leave the crumbs to cool before mixing with the brown sugar. Store in an airtight jar in a cool, dark cupboard.

TO MAKE YOUR EVERYDAY HEALTHY BREAKFAST, pour a portion of low-fat yoghurt into a bowl. Cover with 2 tablespoons of the shaken redcurrants and sprinkle with the rye bread cereal. Enjoy.

Redcurrant and strawberry smoothies *(Serves 4)*

200g redcurrants, de-stalked
300g strawberries, hulled
2 tbsp honey
700ml yoghurt
1 banana, cut into chunks
10 ice cubes

COMBINE ALL THE INGREDIENTS IN A BLENDER and whizz for 3–5 minutes, until smooth. Serve immediately in glasses with a drinking straw in each.

Mackerel is perfect for everyday food in summer as it is inexpensive, healthy and easy to prepare. When you fry mackerel in butter, the skin becomes crisp and tastes delicious. Serve it with a fresh tomato salad and tiny baked potatoes. The dressing here has a sour taste that goes well with the fatty mackerel – if you prefer it sweeter, add some honey.

Fried mackerel with fresh summer salad *(Serves 4)*

4 small fresh mackerel
salt and pepper
30g butter
lemon wedges, to serve

POTATOES
700g small new potatoes
1 lemon, sliced
4 tbsp olive oil

SALAD
4 ripe tomatoes, cut into wedges, then halved
1 cucumber, diced
1 small white salad onion, very finely sliced
2 tbsp white wine vinegar
1 tsp Dijon mustard
a pinch of sugar
4 tbsp olive oil

PREHEAT THE OVEN to 200°C (Gas 6). Put the potatoes in an ovenproof dish with the sliced lemon. Drizzle with the olive oil, sprinkle with salt and freshly ground pepper and mix well. Bake in the oven for 45 minutes.

MEANWHILE, PREPARE THE SALAD. Put the tomatoes, cucumber and onion in a bowl. Mix together the vinegar, mustard, sugar and olive oil and fold the dressing into the salad.

SEASON THE MACKEREL WITH SALT AND PEPPER. Heat the butter in a large frying pan and fry the mackerel for about 5 minutes on each side. Serve the mackerel immediately with the tomato salad, the baked potatoes, and fresh lemon to squeeze over the fish.

When meat is salted, it enhances the flavour and gives a firmer, yet still tender, texture. In summer, I like to serve a lightly salted chicken with fresh tomatoes, which are red and full-flavoured at this time of year. I grow four different kinds of mint in my small urban garden and I therefore use a lot of it in salads, tisanes, and dressings.

Lightly salted chicken with tomato-mint salad and beetroot salad *(Serves 6–8)*

1 large organic chicken

BRINE
1.5 litres water
6 tbsp salt
6 tbsp caster sugar
15 thyme sprigs

BEETROOT SALAD
400g beetroot
2 tbsp olive oil
juice of 1 lime
3 tbsp freshly grated horseradish
1 tsp caster sugar
salt and pepper

TOMATO-MINT SALAD
10 mint leaves
200g small, ripe tomatoes, halved
1 cucumber, diced
1 tbsp virgin olive oil

PUT THE WATER, SALT AND SUGAR in a large saucepan and bring to the boil, whisking until the sugar and salt has dissolved. Turn off the heat and leave the brine to cool before adding the thyme.

TAKE TWO LARGE PLASTIC BAGS AND FIT ONE INSIDE THE OTHER. Put the chicken inside, then pour the brine into the inner bag. Close the inner bag, trying to remove as much of the excess air as possible, then close the outer bag, knotting both securely. Lay the chicken in an ovenproof dish and leave in the refrigerator overnight.

NEXT DAY, PREHEAT THE OVEN to 180°C (Gas 4). Take the chicken out of the bags, wipe it with a paper towel and place it in the ovenproof dish. Roast for 1 hour 30 minutes.

MEANWHILE, PUT THE BEETROOT IN A SAUCEPAN with enough water to cover and boil for 20 minutes or until just tender. Dunk them in cold water and leave them until cool. Peel and cut into cubes. In a mixing bowl, whisk together the oil, lime juice, horseradish, sugar, salt and some freshly ground pepper. Mix the cubed beetroot into the dressing and adjust the seasoning to taste.

FOR THE TOMATO-MINT SALAD, finely chop half the mint leaves, leaving the other five whole. In a bowl, combine the tomatoes, cucumber and both chopped and whole mint leaves. Mix in the olive oil and season with salt and pepper.

WHEN THE CHICKEN IS DONE, carve it into eight portions and serve with the salads.

Rygeost is a very special smoked, soft cheese produced in Denmark. It has the taste of summer sun and is ideal for a light lunch with cold beer.

Smørrebrød: Smoked cheese salad on rye *(Serves 6)*

700g rygeost or
smoked ricotta
200g mayonnaise
(page 92)
200g radishes, coarsely
chopped
½ cucumber, deseeded
and cubed
4 tbsp finely chopped chives
salt and pepper

TO SERVE
rye bread
whole chives
chopped radishes

MIX THE RYGEOST AND MAYONNAISE TOGETHER in a bowl, beating until there are no lumps remaining.

ADD THE RADISHES, CUCUMBER AND CHIVES AND STIR TO MIX. Season to taste with salt and freshly ground pepper, then serve on rye bread, garnished with the whole chives and chopped radishes.

In the good old days it was common to have two-course dinners and that was the main meal of the day. Meat was very expensive, so to make sure nobody went hungry you either had a fruit soup or a 'porridge' such as this before the meal. During the summer, it was fruit porridge served with cold milk or cream. I love this recipe and in my family we enjoy it a great deal during summer both as a pudding and as an afternoon snack.

Fruit 'porridge' with cold cream *(Serves 6)*

1kg redcurrants, destalked
1kg strawberries, hulled
500g raspberries or blackcurrants, destalked
350g caster sugar, plus extra for sprinkling
1 vanilla pod
4 tbsp cornflour
6 tsp ice-cold single cream or milk

RINSE THE REDCURRANTS AND STRAWBERRIES, but do not rinse the raspberries because they are too delicate. If you are using blackcurrants, rinse them and nip off the little brown top. Cut the strawberries into small pieces.

PUT ALL THE FRUIT IN A LARGE SAUCEPAN WITH THE SUGAR AND VANILLA POD. Bring to the boil and skim any froth from the surface, then reduce the heat and leave to simmer for 20 minutes.

DISSOLVE THE CORNFLOUR IN A LITTLE WATER. Raise the heat under the pan and add the cornflour mixture to the porridge, stirring continuously as you bring the pan to the boil. As soon as the porridge reaches boiling point, turn off the heat.

POUR THE FRUIT PORRIDGE INTO A LARGE SERVING BOWL AND LEAVE TO COOL COMPLETELY. Just before serving, sprinkle it with sugar. Serve with ice-cold cream or milk.

This is a fresh and simple pudding that can serve as a light meal or afternoon snack on a summer day. Called kærnemælkskoldskål, this ice-cold soup is a favourite among children and anyone nostalgic for the food of their youth.

Cold buttermilk lemon soup with biscotti *(Serves 4)*

BISCOTTI

250g plain wheat flour
1 tsp baking powder
50g caster sugar
1 tbsp grated organic lemon zest
125g chilled butter, diced
½ beaten egg
50ml whole milk

MAKE THE BISCOTTI – they can be stored in an airtight container for weeks. Sift the flour and baking powder into a bowl and add the sugar and lemon zest. Then rub the butter into the dry ingredients until the mixture resembles breadcrumbs. Add the beaten egg and milk and stir to form a dough.

PREHEAT THE OVEN to 200°C (Gas 6). Knead the dough lightly on a floured work surface, then roll it into a long, thin sausage. Cut the dough into small even-sized pieces and use your hands to shape them into balls about the size of a walnut. Place on two baking trays lined with baking paper and bake for 7 minutes.

BUTTERMILK SOUP

1 vanilla pod
3 organic egg yolks
6 tbsp caster sugar
juice of ½ lemon
2 tbsp grated organic lemon zest
1.5 litres buttermilk
1 whole organic lemon

WHILE THE BISCOTTI ARE STILL HOT, CUT THEM IN TWO. Place them back on the baking trays and bake again at 150°C (Gas 2) for 20 minutes. Leave them to cool on a wire rack then store in an airtight tin.

TO MAKE THE SOUP, split the vanilla pod lengthways and scrape out the seeds with the tip of a knife. In a bowl, beat together the egg yolks, sugar and vanilla seeds until pale and fluffy. Add the lemon juice and zest and the buttermilk. Chill for 1 hour.

CUT THE WHOLE LEMON INTO SLICES and add to the buttermilk soup just before serving. At the table, you crack the biscotti over the soup and eat both immediately.

All Scandinavian cities have a bakery where you can buy freshly baked bread each day and a large range of cakes and layer cakes by the piece. In my family, however, we always have homemade layer cakes for birthdays. It is a good idea to bake the sponge the day before you want to serve the layer cake.

Layer cake with strawberries *(Serves 12)*

SPONGE CAKE
butter, for greasing
3 large eggs
150g caster sugar
110g plain wheat flour
1½ tsp baking powder

PREHEAT THE OVEN to 180°C (Gas 4) and grease a 26cm-diameter cake tin. To make the sponge, beat the eggs and sugar together in an electric mixer for at least for 10 minutes. Sift together the flour and baking powder then fold the dry ingredients gently into the egg mixture. Pour into the cake tin and bake for 25 minutes until the cake springs back when pressed gently in the middle. Leave to cool on a wire rack.

CREAM FILLING
1 vanilla pod
350ml single cream
4 egg yolks
4 tbsp caster sugar
1½ tbsp cornflour
100ml double cream

TO MAKE THE CREAM FILLING, cut the vanilla pod in half lengthways and scrape out the seeds with the tip of a knife. Combine the vanilla seeds and cream in a small saucepan and heat gently. Just before it starts boiling, turn the heat off. In a mixing bowl, whisk the egg yolks, sugar and cornflour together until pale and fluffy.

POUR A THIRD OF THE HOT CREAM ONTO THE EGG MIXTURE, whisking well. Pour the egg mixture into the saucepan and stir it into the remaining cream. Turn the heat back on. Whisk the mixture over a low heat until it thickens, but do not let it boil. Once the mixture thickens, remove it from the heat and leave to cool. Whip the double cream until very stiff, then fold it into the cooled vanilla cream.

FRUIT FILLING
2kg strawberries, hulled and quartered
500g redcurrants, half de-stalked
icing sugar, for dusting

CUT THE SPONGE CAKE INTO THREE LAYERS and place the bottom piece on a serving plate. Spread half the cream over it, then add half the strawberries and half the destalked redcurrants. Add another layer of sponge, the rest of the cream and the rest of the prepared fruit. Cover with the last piece of sponge, dust with icing sugar and decorate with the reserved redcurrants on their stalks. Serve with tea and coffee.

August

There are a number of archipelagos in Norway and Sweden, such as that around Stockholm. The islands are typically very rocky, with cliffs, valleys, lakes and bays. The seascape is idyllic, calm and very beautiful. In August the weather is always nice. That is, at least, the way I remember it. In the kitchen it is the time for mackerel, crayfish, dill, tomatoes, gooseberries and even more redcurrants.

The crayfish season is short: about 3 weeks in August. Furthermore, the Swedish crayfish are rare and expensive. People tend to boil them in beer and eat them outside in the garden with aquavit and beer. It is a wonderful way to celebrate life. I cook them in the morning and leave them to cool in the pot, then I pack a picnic basket and go down to the little lake near the house in Sweden where I often stay. It is so quiet and blissful that you almost forget everything around you and slip into a time-free zone.

Crayfish with bread and mayo *(Serves 6)*

6 litres water
1.5 litres dark beer such as stout or brown ale
5 dill sprigs, plus extra to garnish
125g salt
50g caster sugar
2 tbsp whole peppercorns
2 tbsp coriander seeds
1 lemon, sliced
3kg live crayfish

TO SERVE
herb mayonnaise (page 94)
rye bread
crisp green salad

PUT ALL THE INGREDIENTS except for the crayfish in a large pot and bring to the boil. Once boiling, add the crayfish and return to the boil. Let it boil hard for 1 minute, then turn the heat off and leave the fish in the pot until the liquid is cold.

DRAIN THE CRAYFISH and serve them cold, garnished with dill and accompanied by homemade herb mayo, rye bread, crisp green salad, beer and aquavit.

This Scandinavian speciality can be made in hundreds of different ways. Fishcakes are suitable for dinner the day they are prepared, or served cold the next day with a salad or on rye bread. The remoulade is a must, and best when homemade. Many different types of fish can be used for fishcakes, but it is important that the fish used is raw.

Fishcakes with herb remoulade and dill potatoes *(Serves 4)*

HERB REMOULADE
1 tbsp cornichons
1 tsp capers
200g mayonnaise (page 92)
3 tbsp half-fat crème fraîche
1 tsp Dijon mustard
1 tsp curry powder
2 tbsp chopped chives
2 tbsp chopped tarragon
2 tbsp finely chopped carrots
1 tbsp lemon juice
salt and pepper

FISHCAKES
600g white fish fillets
2 spring onions, chopped
2 eggs
100ml single cream
2 tbsp finely chopped tarragon
3 tbsp finely chopped parsley
juice of ½ lemon
2 tbsp potato flour
30g butter
vegetable oil, for frying
dill sprigs, to garnish

POTATOES
50g butter
800g cold boiled fingerling potatoes, peeled
4 tbsp chopped dill

START WITH THE REMOULADE. Chop the cornichons and capers together, then place in a mixing bowl with the remaining ingredients. Stir well and season to taste with salt and freshly ground pepper. Cover and put in the refrigerator until ready to serve.

TO MAKE THE FISHCAKES, chop the fish fillets finely with a very sharp knife. Put in a mixing bowl with the spring onions, eggs, cream, herbs and lemon juice and fold together gently. Add the potato flour, 2 teaspoons of salt and 1 teaspoon of pepper and fold again.

HEAT THE BUTTER AND VEGETABLE OIL TOGETHER IN A LARGE FRYING PAN. Meanwhile, shape the fish mixture into 12 small balls using a spoon and your hands. Gently place the fishcakes in the pan and fry over a medium heat for about 4 minutes on each side.

MEANWHILE, IN ANOTHER FRYING PAN, melt the butter for cooking the potatoes. When it starts to bubble, add the potatoes and fry them slowly until golden. Fold in the chopped dill.

SERVE THE POTATOES WITH THE FISHCAKES AND HERB REMOULADE, garnishing the fishcakes with dill sprigs. A green salad would also be perfect here, or the sweet and sour cucumber salad on page 86.

Eggs are an important everyday food in many cultures. We have, for example, soft-boiled eggs for breakfast, and hard-boiled eggs on rye bread for lunch. We also eat a simple omelette called æggekage, which is like a Spanish omelette without the potato. With bacon, chives and fresh tomatoes on the side, this dish is served for lunch and dinner in summer, when the chives are cut from the garden and the tomatoes are ripe and tasteful. It would also be perfect for brunch.

Omelettes with tomatoes, bacon and chives *(Serves 4)*

8 large organic eggs
100ml whole milk
1 tsp plain wheat flour
salt and pepper
25g butter or 2 tbsp olive oil
12 pieces thickly sliced organic bacon, 5–8cm long, preferably hand-cut
4 tomatoes, sliced
4 tbsp finely chopped chives
4 slices rye bread

BREAK THE EGGS into a large bowl and beat them thoroughly. Mix in the milk, flour and some salt and freshly ground pepper and beat again until there are no lumps left.

DIVIDE THE BUTTER or oil between four small lidded frying pans (or you could cook just one large omelettte) and place over a medium heat. Add the egg mixture and let it cook for 2 minutes, then turn the heat down to very low. Put the lids over the pans and cook for 8 minutes. (If cooking the mixture as one large omelette, cook for 5 and 12 minutes respectively.)

MEANWHILE, GRILL OR FRY THE BACON until golden and crisp. Place the sliced tomatoes and bacon on the omelettes, sprinkle with the chives, and serve with the rye bread. A cold beer is also very nice with this dish.

The classic dish kalvespidsbryst is normally served with gravy, but this summer version still has lots of flavour and works well served with vegetables. If there are any leftovers, slice the meat and serve it on rye bread with mustard and pickled cucumbers.

Veal brisket with sautéed vegetables *(Serves 4)*

1.5kg veal brisket
500ml dry white wine
500ml water
1 tbsp whole peppercorns
1 tbsp sea salt
3 shallots
1 leek, sliced
10 thyme sprigs
3 garlic cloves
3 dill sprigs
3 carrots
1 tbsp coarse sea salt
5 bay leaves

VEGETABLES
4 tbsp olive oil
2 garlic cloves, finely chopped
200g mushrooms, quartered
500g broccoli florets, quartered or halved, depending on size
4 tomatoes
salt and pepper
50g horseradish, grated

POTATOES
1kg potatoes
4 tbsp olive oil

PUT THE VEAL IN A LARGE SAUCEPAN, pour over the wine and water, then add all the vegetables and flavourings. Bring to the boil and skim any froth from the surface. Reduce the heat to a simmer, half-cover the pan and let it cook gently for 2½ hours.

PREHEAT THE OVEN to 200°C (Gas 6) half an hour before the veal will be ready. Cook the potatoes in a large pan of salted water until tender, then drain. Slice the potatoes and put them in an ovenproof dish. Stir in the olive oil and sprinkle with salt and freshly ground pepper. Roast in the oven for 15 minutes.

MEANWHILE, FOR THE VEGETABLES, heat the olive oil in a large sauté pan and fry the garlic and mushrooms together for 2 minutes. Add the broccoli florets and cook for 5 minutes. Take 100ml broth from the meat and add it to the sauté pan along with the tomatoes. Simmer for 3 minutes then season to taste with salt and pepper.

CAREFULLY LIFT THE MEAT FROM THE BROTH AND PLACE IT ON A CUTTING BOARD. Carve it in slices and arrange on a serving dish. Cover the meat with the vegetables and sprinkle the horseradish over the top. Serve with the potatoes alongside.

Although this dish originates in Vienna, it has become a classic served throughout Europe and illustrates the extent to which European countries have influenced each other in developing food culture. It is important, I think, to broaden your horizons and at the same time preserve tradition. When it comes to food, I believe you have to be familiar with your own cuisine but also keep developing it to a modern and healthy standard.

Wienerschnitzel with braised potatoes *(Serves 4)*

700g potatoes
4 thin veal escalopes
200g fresh breadcrumbs
salt and pepper
2 eggs
100g butter
4 lemon slices
8 anchovy fillets
2 tbsp capers

BOIL THE POTATOES IN A LARGE PAN of salted water until just tender, then drain them. When they are cool enough to handle, peel them and keep them warm.

IF THE VEAL ESCALOPES ARE NOT ALREADY PAPER-THIN, beat each one with the flat of a heavy knife or a meat mallet.

PUT THE BREADCRUMBS ON A WIDE DISH OR PLATE and season with salt and freshly ground pepper. Beat the eggs together in a bowl. Dip the escalopes one at a time into the beaten eggs until completely coated, then lay them in the breadcrumbs and press the crumbs into the veal until evenly coated.

DIVIDE 50G OF THE BUTTER BETWEEN TWO FRYING PANS and heat until melted. When hot, add the wienerschnitzel – two to each pan – and cook for about 3 minutes on each side. Make sure that they stay golden and do not start to turn dark brown – if necessary, lower the heat.

LIFT THE WIENERSCHNITZEL FROM THE PANS and set aside in a warm place. Add the remaining butter to the pans and allow it to melt, being careful not to burn it. Add the potatoes to the pans, stir gently to coat, then season with pepper.

ARRANGE THE WIENERSCHNITZEL ON FOUR PLATES. Place a slice of lemon, two anchovy fillets and some capers on each one and serve immediately with the potatoes and butter sauce.

In August, there are so many soft fruits to choose from, and a perfect way to eat them is with vanilla parfait. It is easier to prepare than an ice cream, because you do not have to cook the cream, use an ice-cream machine or go through the hassle of stirring every 15 minutes while the mixture is freezing. It can also be prepared days ahead of serving.

Vanilla parfait with redcurrants *(Serves 4)*

1 vanilla pod
6 egg yolks
125g caster sugar
800ml double cream
100g redcurrants

SLIT THE VANILLA POD LENGTHWAYS and scrape out the seeds with the tip of a knife. Put the seeds in a bowl with the egg yolks and sugar and beat until pale and fluffy. Whip the double cream until it forms soft peaks, then very gently fold it into the egg mixture.

POUR THE MIXTURE INTO ONE OR MORE FREEZER-PROOF CONTAINERS and freeze for 6 hours. The parfait is now ready. Serve with redcurrants or other fresh fruit on a summer day.

All summer I look forward to August because it is the season for gooseberries, which I buy in shops or collect in my mother's garden. I boil them with sugar and vanilla to make a compote, then eat them with crêpes (super-thin pancakes). When I make crêpes, I like to cook a big pile so that it seems they will last forever.

Crêpes with gooseberry compote *(Serves 8)*

COMPOTE
1 vanilla pod
500g unripe gooseberries, trimmed
200g caster sugar

PANCAKES
4 eggs
300ml buttermilk
1 vanilla pod
250g plain wheat flour
2 tsp caster sugar
1 tsp salt
300ml whole milk
butter, for frying

TO MAKE THE COMPOTE, halve the vanilla pod lengthways and place in a saucepan with the gooseberries and sugar. Bring to the boil, then lower the heat and leave to simmer for 30 minutes. Pour the hot compote into sterilized preserving jars, seal tightly and, when cool, store in the refrigerator.

FOR THE CRÊPE BATTER, beat the eggs together in a large mixing bowl. Add the buttermilk and beat again. Slit the vanilla pod in half lengthways and scrape out the seeds with the tip of a knife. Sift the flour, sugar and salt together, then add to the egg mixture and beat until smooth. Stir in the milk and vanilla seeds and leave the batter to rest for 30 minutes before cooking the crêpes.

MELT A LITTLE BUTTER IN A FRYING PAN. When hot, add half a ladle of batter to the pan, twisting the handle gently to make a large, thin crêpe. Fry until golden on each side – it takes about 2 minutes. Set aside and repeat with the remaining batter. Stack the pancakes on a plate, interleaving them with greaseproof paper. They will stay warm like this for some time but, if you prefer, you can put them in a low oven. When the crêpes are all done, serve with the gooseberry compote.

September

Late summer or early autumn is a beautiful time to visit Stockholm. The sunlight is still

warm and it does not get dark until 8 o'clock. You can still sit outside on some evenings.

It is time for tasty blueberries and earthy chanterelles, it is time to make preserves for

winter and it is – because of the changing weather – time for simmered dishes.

This is an easy way to make a very tasty pâté for lunch. Serve it with rye bread and preserved cucumber. It is also perfect as part of a buffet.

Chicken liver pâté with aquavit *(Serves 8)*

30g butter
1 onion, chopped
3 garlic cloves, chopped
1kg chicken livers, trimmed and halved
10 thyme sprigs
200ml aquavit
250g chilled butter, cubed
250ml half-fat crème fraîche
2 tbsp coarsely chopped mixed whole peppercorns
salt and pepper

HEAT THE BUTTER IN A LARGE SAUCEPAN, add the onion and garlic and sauté until soft. Add the chicken livers and thyme and cook for 10 minutes, stirring occasionally.

ADD THE AQUAVIT, raise the heat and simmer for 2 minutes. Turn off the heat and leave the mixture in the saucepan for 5 minutes. Take out the thyme sprigs, then transfer the chicken liver mixture to a food processor.

ADD THE BUTTER, CRÈME FRAÎCHE AND PEPPERCORNS AND BLEND UNTIL SMOOTH. Season to taste with salt and freshly ground pepper. Pour the pâté mixture into a terrine or loaf tin and place in the refrigerator until the next day.

SERVE THE PÂTÉ with pickled cucumber or beetroot (see overleaf), toasted bread or rye bread.

Cucumbers are easily preserved and taste wonderful on smørrebrød. They can be enjoyed with cold meats and mustard, with various cooked meat dishes, or in burgers. Pickled beetroot can be eaten with smørrebrød, served as a condiment for Captain's stew, or chopped and stirred into Biff Lindström (pages 52 and 54).

Pickled cucumbers *(Makes 1 litre)*

3–4 cucumbers, cut into 2cm slices
1 large dill sprig, separated into florets

IN A LARGE SAUCEPAN BRING THE VINEGAR, SUGAR AND SALT TO THE BOIL, whisking until the sugar has dissolved. Turn the heat off, add the lemon juice and leave to cool.

PACK THE CUCUMBERS AND DILL into a sterilized 1-litre jar, pressing them together.

BRINE
1 litre spirit vinegar
400g caster sugar
2½ tsp salt
juice of 2 lemons
1 tbsp whole peppercorns

POUR THE SPICED VINEGAR OVER THE CUCUMBER AND SEAL TIGHTLY. Next day there will be room in the jar to pack in more cucumbers. Do this, then leave to rest until the next day, when they will be ready to serve.

STORE THE PICKLES IN A DARK CUPBOARD UNTIL OPENING; thereafter keep them in the refrigerator and use within 2 months.

Pickled beetroot with star anise *(Makes 1 litre)*

1kg small beetroot
salt

PEEL THE BEETROOT AND BOIL THEM IN SALTED WATER for about 20 minutes – maybe a little less. Check them after 10 minutes: they have to have some bite and are best if not too soft.

BRINE
750ml spirit vinegar
400g caster sugar
1 star anise
1 tbsp whole peppercorns

WHILE THE BEETROOT ARE BOILING, make the brine. Bring the vinegar, sugar, star anise and peppercorns to the boil in a saucepan, whisking until the sugar has dissolved. Turn the heat off and leave to cool.

DRAIN THE COOKED BEETROOT and, when cool enough to handle, cut into 5mm slices. Pack them in a sterilized jar, pressing them together, pour over the brine and seal tightly. Leave to rest for one week before serving.

I love salmon, and this is the perfect way to eat it: served with this sauce (called fox sauce) and fresh dill, with an ice-cold beer alongside.

Gravad lax with honey mustard sauce *(Serves 8–10)*

1 salmon fillet, about 2.5kg
2 tbsp whole peppercorns
1 tbsp coriander seeds
120g coarse salt
170g caster sugar
200g dill, very finely chopped, plus 6 sprigs extra

SAUCE
3 tbsp dark brown sugar
3 tbsp Dijon mustard
3 tbsp white wine vinegar
2 tbsp vegetable oil
100g dill, chopped

FREEZE THE SALMON FOR 24 HOURS before making the gravad lax to ensure there are no harmful bacteria, then defrost it.

REMOVE ANY PIN-BONES FROM THE SALMON and trim the edges of the fillet. Wipe off any scales with a paper towel and lay the salmon skin-side down on a sheet of cling film.

CRUSH THE PEPPERCORNS AND CORIANDER SEEDS USING A PESTLE AND MORTAR and mix with the salt and sugar. Spread the finely chopped dill evenly over the salmon, then cover with the spiced sugar mixture. Cut the salmon into two equal portions. Lay three of the dill sprigs over one piece then cover with the other piece of fish, laying it flesh-side down. Wrap in cling film and leave for 2 days in the refrigerator.

TO MAKE THE SAUCE, place all the ingredients in a blender or food processor and whizz until the mixture is smooth.

TO SERVE, unwrap the salmon and wipe off all the salt and sugar mixture with a paper towel. The traditional cut starts diagonally at one corner of the salmon, and then works back towards the centre of the fillet. Place the gravad lax on a serving dish and garnish with the remaining dill sprigs. Serve with the honey mustard sauce and white or spelt bread.

In September, the weather can be everything from cold and rainy to an Indian summer. On rainy days, when it gets a bit gloomy, I like to start some slow cooking – it gives me tremendous comfort when the aroma fills the kitchen and I'm reminded why I love living in a place with changing seasons.

Lamb shanks with apricots and spices and parsley mash (Serves 4)

4 small lamb shanks
4 tbsp olive oil
500ml red wine
100g dried organic apricots
3 shallots, roughly chopped
3 garlic cloves, roughly chopped
1 cinnamon stick
10 whole cloves
2 rosemary sprigs
1 tbsp grated organic lemon zest, plus extra to garnish
2 carrots, peeled
1 parsnip, peeled
1 turnip, peeled
1 tbsp salt
1 tbsp whole peppercorns

MASH
1.5kg large potatoes
1 tsp freshly grated mace
6 tbsp finely chopped parsley
4 tbsp olive oil
25g butter
salt and pepper

IN A LARGE CHEF'S PAN OR CASSEROLE, brown the lamb shanks in the oil until they are golden brown all over. Add the red wine, apricots, shallots, garlic, spices, rosemary, lemon zest and enough water to partially cover the lamb. Bring to the boil and skim any froth that rises to the surface. Add some salt and freshly ground pepper, then reduce the heat to a gentle simmer, cover and leave to cook for 2 hours.

TO MAKE THE MASH, peel and cube the potatoes and boil them in salted water until tender. Drain, reserving some of the cooking liquid. Put the potatoes in a large bowl with the mace, parsley, olive oil and butter and use a balloon whisk to mash the potatoes until the texture is only slightly lumpy. Add a little bit of the potato cooking water if the mash is not soft enough. Season to taste with salt and pepper.

CUT THE CARROTS, PARSNIP AND TURNIP INTO LARGE CHUNKS AND ADD TO THE LAMB. Leave to simmer for 15 minutes more, then season to taste with salt and pepper. Put the lamb shanks on a serving dish with the vegetables and apricots, garnish with lemon zest and serve with the mash.

Horseradish has a very special sharp, peppery taste that is highly versatile. It can be used in sauces and dressings, or just shredded and sprinkled on a cold piece of meat with mustard and served on a slice of bread. Horseradish grows very well in our climate. If you can't find chervil for the sauce, use parsley.

Chicken in horseradish and chervil sauce *(Serves 4)*

1 whole chicken
1 small whole onion
1 carrot
3 bay leaves
1 tbsp whole peppercorns
1 tbsp coarse salt
1kg boiled potatoes, to serve

SAUCE
20g butter
400g Jerusalem artichokes, peeled and finely sliced
1 fennel bulb, sliced
1 tbsp plain wheat flour
600ml chicken broth (from cooking chicken)
6 tbsp freshly grated horseradish
200ml double cream
4 tbsp chopped chervil
salt and pepper

PUT THE CHICKEN IN A LARGE CASSEROLE with the onion, carrot, bay leaves, peppercorns and salt. Add enough water to cover the chicken, then bring to the boil and simmer for 1 hour. Carefully lift the chicken from the broth and leave to cool. Strain the broth and save 600ml for the sauce.

MELT THE BUTTER IN A LARGE SAUCEPAN. Add the sliced artichokes and fennel and cook for 2 minutes. Sprinkle the flour over the vegetables and stir until the flour and butter have combined. Pour in half the chicken broth and stir until smooth. Add the remaining chicken broth and the horseradish and bring to the boil. Add the cream and some salt and freshly ground pepper and return the sauce to the boil, then reduce the heat to a simmer.

REMOVE ALL THE CHICKEN FLESH FROM THE BONES and divide it into medium-sized pieces. Stir the chicken and chervil into the sauce and let it simmer for a couple of minutes or until the chicken is hot through. Season to taste with salt and pepper and serve with boiled potatoes.

The chanterelle season starts in late August and, if it is a good year, goes on until October. The best ones are collected in the woods. In Denmark we have professional pickers who, after they have been to the woods, will sell the chanterelles directly to stores and restaurants. Chanterelles are ruined if you wash them in water; brushing them clean is a lot of work, but worth it.

Chanterelle, bacon and plum salad with blue cheese *(Serves 4)*

200g organic bacon, cubed
200g chanterelles
2 tbsp olive oil
salt and pepper
10 red or green plums, stoned and cut into wedges
200g mixed lettuce leaves
135g blue cheese, crumbled

DRESSING
4 tbsp balsamic vinegar
½ tsp caster sugar
2 tbsp olive oil

COOK THE BACON UNTIL GOLDEN IN A FRYING PAN. Leave to drain on a piece of paper towel.

USE A DRY BRUSH TO CLEAN THE CHANTERELLES, then fry them for 5 minutes in 1 tablespoon of the olive oil. Season with salt and freshly ground pepper and leave to cool in the frying pan.

SAUTÉ THE PLUMS FOR A MINUTE in the remaining oil.

TO MAKE THE DRESSING, mix the balsamic vinegar and sugar together in a small bowl, then whisk in the olive oil until the mixture has emulsified (this will take a while as there is more vinegar than oil).

JUST BEFORE SERVING, combine the bacon, mushrooms, plums and lettuce. Pour the dressing over and toss gently. Add the blue cheese but do not toss the salad any more because it easily turns mushy.

SCANDINAVIAN CHEESE PLATTER. Knäkebröd is a very healthy flatbread and this version, made with rye flour, is easy to make at home. It is perfect with cheese, and a great snack with honey, and will keep in an airtight container for up to a week.

Rye flatbread *(Makes 10)*

50g fresh yeast
500ml lukewarm water
1 tsp salt
2 tsp aniseed
1 tbsp honey
100ml sunflower oil
200g rye flour
200g rolled oats
250g plain wheat flour

DISSOLVE THE YEAST IN THE WARM WATER, then add the salt, aniseed, honey and oil and mix well. Add the rye flour, oats and half the wheat flour and mix for 5 minutes if using an electric mixer, or for 10 minutes if making the dough by hand. Sprinkle the rest of the wheat flour over the dough and leave it to rise for 15 minutes.

PREHEAT THE OVEN to 220°C (Gas 7) and line a baking sheet with baking paper. Knead the dough on a floured work surface, then divide it into ten equal pieces and roll each one into a very thin disc. Lay the flatbreads on the baking paper and bake for 5–8 minutes until crisp.

Walnuts in wine

100g caster sugar
100ml water
100ml dessert wine, port, sherry or red or white wine
150g shelled walnuts

PUT THE SUGAR AND WATER IN A SAUCEPAN and bring to the boil, stirring to dissolve the sugar, then reduce the heat and leave to simmer for 5 minutes. Add the wine and continue simmering for about 10 minutes, stirring occasionally, until the mixture develops a syrupy consistency.

MEANWHILE, IN A SEPARATE SAUCEPAN, boil the walnuts in a generous amount of water for 1 minute, then drain them. Mix the syrup and walnuts together and store in a sterilized jar until serving. Kept in the refrigerator, they can last for up to a month.

Scandinavian cheeses

SCT CLEMMENS BLUE CHEESE FROM DENMARK
A lovely blue cheese produced on an island called Bornholm, it is made from cows' milk and has a mild, creamy taste.

JARLSBERG FROM NORWAY
This cows' milk cheese has a sweet, nutty taste. It is perfect in sandwiches or melted in burgers, used in salads or simply served with a flatbread and a glass of red wine.

VÄSTERBOTTEN FROM SWEDEN
A hard and dry cheese with a salty taste, it is suitable for pies, grating or serving on flatbreads with sweet walnuts.

We gather wild blueberries in the woods. The best way to eat them is fresh with a bowl of yoghurt, or in a tart served warm with cold crème fraîche.

Blueberry tart *(Serves 10)*

PASTRY
350g plain wheat flour
100g icing sugar
100g chilled butter, cubed
1 whole egg plus 1 egg yolk
butter, for greasing

FILLING
1kg blueberries
125g caster sugar

500ml low-fat crème fraîche, to serve

TO MAKE THE PASTRY, sift the flour and icing sugar together into a bowl. Rub the butter into the dry ingredients with your fingertips until the mixture resembles breadcrumbs. Add the whole egg and yolk and stir until the pastry comes together.

KNEAD THE PASTRY LIGHTLY ON A FLOURED WORK SURFACE. Shape into a ball, wrap in cling film and leave to rest in the refrigerator for 1 hour.

LIGHTLY BUTTER a 26cm-diameter tart tin. Roll out the pastry thinly on a lightly floured work surface and use the pastry to line the tart tin. Trim the edges and leave to rest again in the refrigerator for 1 hour.

PREHEAT THE OVEN to 180°C (Gas 4). Cover the pastry with a circle of baking paper and weigh it down with dry beans or rice. Bake for 20 minutes. Take the tart case out of the oven and remove the baking paper and beans. Return the tart case to the oven for another 10 minutes.

TO MAKE THE FILLING, rinse the blueberries and mix them with the sugar. Remove the pastry case from the oven and increase the oven temperature to 200°C (Gas 6). Pour the blueberries into the pastry case and return to the oven for 20 minutes.

REMOVE THE TART FROM THE OVEN and let it cool for 10 minutes before serving with crème fraîche.

October

The season changes. The foliage of trees in woods and cities turns red, yellow and brown, and autumn leaves pile up under the trees. The sky is very beautiful with alternating clouds and sunshine. Days begin to shorten and the shades of daylight are shifting once again, this time to greyish colours. It is time for game, root vegetables, apples, hazelnuts and walnuts – everything that gives comfort and pleasure. It is time to cook, and to tuck in.

In Scandinavia hot meals are frequently served with potatoes. They were consumed almost every day before rice and pasta were introduced. My grandparents had potatoes almost every day of their life. But during winter, I get tired of eating boiled potatoes, and potato soup is, therefore, a nice alternative. Instead of bacon you can use crisp croutons of dark rye bread.

Potato soup with bacon and chives *(Serves 4)*

1.3kg potatoes, peeled and cut into large chunks
2 leeks, sliced
2 garlic cloves
2 bay leaves
1 tbsp salt
1 tbsp whole peppercorns
1 litre water
100ml double cream

TO SERVE
100g bacon, diced
4 tbsp chopped chives
grainy bread

PLACE THE POTATOES IN A LARGE SAUCEPAN with the leeks, garlic, bay leaves, salt, peppercorns and water. Bring to the boil, the reduce the heat and leave to simmer for 20 minutes.

WHILE THE SOUP IS COOKING, fry the bacon until crisp and golden, then leave to drain on paper towels to remove the excess fat.

REMOVE THE SOUP FROM THE HEAT AND LIFT OUT THE BAY LEAVES. Purée the mixture in a blender or food processor then return it to the saucepan. Add the cream and heat through. Adjust the seasoning to taste, then serve the soup very hot with the bacon and chives, plus grainy bread on the side.

This is an old recipe that has survived many generations, a wholesome and tasty meal that I prepare once every winter. The flavour is enhanced if the ragout is made the day before you serve it. If there are only four of you, you can serve it for dinner on two nights.

Oxtail ragout (Serves 8)

2kg oxtail pieces
100g butter
4 tbsp olive oil
1 tbsp plain wheat flour
500ml red wine
4 shallots, roughly chopped
6 garlic cloves, roughly chopped
2 rosemary sprigs
4 bay leaves
1 tbsp whole peppercorns
1 tbsp coarse salt

TO SERVE
5 parsnips, peeled and cut into long strips
4 tbsp olive oil
200g chanterelles
30g butter
few sprigs flat-leaf parsley, to garnish

TRIM ANY EXCESS FAT from the oxtail and dry with paper towels. Melt the butter in a large, heavy-based casserole, then add the oil and brown the oxtail, turning so they take on a nice golden colour all over. Work in batches if you need to.

SPRINKLE THE FLOUR OVER the oxtail and turn until the flour is absorbed. Pour in the red wine, stir again, then add the shallots, garlic, rosemary, bay leaves, peppercorns and salt. Add enough water to almost cover the oxtail and bring to the boil. Skim any froth that forms on the surface, then reduce the heat, cover and leave to simmer for 3 hours.

ABOUT HALF AN HOUR BEFORE the oxtail will be ready, preheat the oven to 200°C (Gas 6). For the vegetable accompaniments, place the parsnips in an ovenproof dish, add the olive oil, turn until coated and sprinkle with salt and freshly ground pepper. Roast for 20 minutes.

CLEAN THE CHANTERELLES WITH A DRY BRUSH then fry them in the butter for 5 minutes. When the ragout is cooked, serve it with the chanterelles, roast parsnips and fresh parsley. You can also serve it with mashed potatoes.

Ham is traditional in Scandinavia, just as it is in Spain and Italy, but we are not as famous for it as they are. However, our hams are also of excellent quality and their salty taste goes well with this cheese tart. Skagen ham from Denmark is lightly smoked.

Swedish cheese tart with ham *(Serves 4)*

about 250g puff pastry
butter, for greasing
4 eggs
150ml whole milk
300g Västerbotten cheese,
or strong hard cheese such
as Cheddar, grated
½ tsp salt
pepper

TO SERVE
12 thin slices Skagen ham,
or Serrano or Parma ham
green salad

PREHEAT THE OVEN to 180°C (Gas 4). Roll out the pasty on a floured work surface until thin then use it to line a buttered 20cm-diameter tart tin (preferably one with a perforated base to help make the pastry crunchy).

IN A BOWL, BEAT THE EGGS AND MILK and stir in the cheese, salt and lots of freshly ground pepper. Pour the mixture into the tart case.

BAKE FOR 45 MINUTES, then serve the tart warm with the ham and a crisp green salad.

Reindeer fillet is very tender and low in fat and the taste is similar to moose. I like to add a bit of spice to it by covering it with lots of ground pepper and anise. Reindeer live in the northern part of Scandinavia and in this recipe you can replace reindeer with any kind of venison. I do not recommend serving reindeer well done because it tends to be dry – medium-rare is best.

Reindeer with anise and pepper, potato-celeriac gratin and Brussels sprouts *(Serves 4)*

GRATIN

600g potatoes, peeled and cut into large cubes

400g celeriac, peeled and cut into large cubes

2 garlic cloves

3 rosemary sprigs

1 tbsp whole peppercorns

1 tbsp salt

70g butter

100g Cheddar cheese, grated

100ml double cream

REINDEER

800g reindeer fillet

1 tbsp aniseed

1 tbsp whole peppercorns

olive oil, for frying

TO SERVE

500g Brussels sprouts, halved

cowberry compote (see page 84) or redcurrant jelly

TO MAKE THE GRATIN, place the potatoes and celeriac in a large saucepan with the garlic, rosemary, peppercorns and salt. Cover generously with water, bring to the boil and cook for 30 minutes. Drain, reserving some of the cooking liquid.

PREHEAT THE OVEN to 200°C (Gas 6). Discard the rosemary sprigs and mash the potatoes and celeriac with a balloon whisk. While the mixture is still lumpy, add 50g of the butter, plus the cheese and cream. Stir again – this time with a spoon – and season with salt and freshly ground pepper. Divide the mash between four small buttered soufflé dishes, or put it all in one large dish. Bake for 10 minutes or, if you are making this in advance and you have let the mash go cold, bake for 30 minutes.

MEANWHILE, HEAT THE REMAINING BUTTER IN A FRYING PAN and fry the sprouts for 5 minutes. Sprinkle with salt and pepper and keep warm.

CUT THE REINDEER FILLET INTO EIGHT EQUAL SLICES. Use a pestle and mortar to crush the aniseed and peppercorns and place them on a dish. Turn the reindeer in it to coat evenly.

HEAT THE OLIVE OIL IN A FRYING PAN and cook the reindeer slices for 3–4 minutes on each side so that they will be medium-rare. Serve with the gratin, Brussels sprouts and cowberry compote or redcurrant jelly.

AUTUMN SALADS. There are many ways to combine all the wonderful fruits and vegetables of autumn – the only limit is your imagination. Hamburg parsley is a highly popular root vegetable in Denmark that looks rather like parsnip; if you can't find any, substitute it with celeriac.

Baked root vegetable salad *(Serves 4)*

2 beetroot
2 carrots
½ celeriac
2 parsnips
2 Hamburg parsleys
4 tbsp olive oil
salt and pepper
4 tbsp balsamic vinegar

PREHEAT THE OVEN to 180°C (Gas 4). Peel all the vegetables and cut them lengthways into strips. Place in a roasting tray, pour the olive oil over and sprinkle with salt and freshly ground pepper. Use your hands to mix the root vegetables in the oil, then roast for 30 minutes.

WHEN THE VEGETABLES ARE DONE, transfer them to a serving bowl and stir in the balsamic vinegar. Adjust the seasoning to taste with salt and pepper, then serve warm or cold.

Spelt salad *(Serves 4)*

200g whole spelt grains
½ celeriac, peeled and diced
4 tbsp olive oil
4 tbsp finely chopped flat-leafed parsley
6 tbsp chopped curly parsley
4 tbsp finely chopped chives
2 tbsp white wine vinegar
salt and pepper

SOAK THE SPELT GRAINS IN A BOWL OF COLD WATER for 1 hour, then drain. Place in a saucepan and, cover with fresh water, bring to the boil and cook for 30 minutes. Drain and leave to cool.

MEANWHILE, PREHEAT THE OVEN to 180°C (Gas 4). Roast the celeriac in the olive oil for about 20 minutes until tender. While the celeriac is still hot, mix it into the cooked spelt and leave to cool.

ADD THE CHOPPED HERBS AND WHITE WINE VINEGAR, and season with salt and freshly ground pepper before serving.

Jerusalem artichoke salad *(Serves 4–6)*

600g Jerusalem artichokes
3 lemon slices
100g walnuts, dried or fresh
1 tsp Dijon mustard
1 tsp caster sugar
2 tbsp cider vinegar
4 tbsp walnut oil
200g green grapes, halved and deseeded
salt and pepper

HAVE READY A BOWL OF WATER WITH THE LEMON SLICES. Peel the Jerusalem artichokes and cut them into very thin slices, adding them to the water as you go to prevent browning.

CHOP THE WALNUTS ROUGHLY. In a small bowl, whisk together the mustard, sugar, vinegar and walnut oil to make a dressing.

DRAIN THE JERUSALEM ARTICHOKES WELL and place in a bowl with the grapes and walnuts. Fold in the dressing, season with salt and freshly ground pepper and serve immediately.

This is (still) the best apple pudding I have ever had and it is served cold. Apple is the dominating flavour but the pudding has a crunchy edge from caramelized croutons.

Apple trifle *(Serves 8)*

1.5kg cooking apples such as Bramleys, peeled, cored and cubed
175g caster sugar
1 vanilla pod
200g stale bread, diced
50g butter
200ml double cream

PLACE THE APPLE CUBES IN A SAUCEPAN. Cut the vanilla pod lengthways, then scrape the seeds out with the tip of a knife and add to the apples with 100g of the caster sugar. Bring to the boil, then reduce the heat and leave to simmer for 10 minutes. Stir the mixture to give a lumpy apple sauce then leave to cool.

TOAST THE BREAD PIECES IN A DRY FRYING PAN, stirring frequently, until they begin to take on some colour. Add the butter and remaining sugar and continue cooking and stirring so that the tiny croutons caramelize slowly and evenly, without burning.

IN A SERVING BOWL, preferably a glass one, alternative layers of apple sauce and croutons. Whip the cream until it forms soft peaks and use it to decorate the top of the dessert. Eat immediately or let it rest in the refrigerator for a couple of hours before serving.

You can buy soft, sweet cinnamon rolls all over Scandinavia in different variations, but the home-baked ones are the best, of course. They are perfect for a late breakfast or afternoon tea, or served with the hot apple drink below. I think hot drinks such as this are very romantic – the essence of everything that autumn has to offer.

Cinnamon rolls *(Makes 18–20)*

50g fresh yeast
500ml lukewarm milk
150g softened butter
1 egg, beaten
850g plain wheat flour
½ tsp salt
150g caster sugar
2 tsp ground cardamom

FILLING
150g soft butter
100g caster sugar
4 tsp ground cinnamon

GLAZE
1 egg, beaten
caster sugar, for sprinkling

IN A LARGE BOWL, DISSOLVE THE YEAST IN THE WARM MILK USING A WOODEN SPOON. Mix in the butter, then add the egg and stir again. Sift together the flour, salt and cardamom and add to the milk mixture with the sugar, stirring to form a dough. Keep stirring until the dough comes cleanly from the edge of the bowl.

KNEAD THE DOUGH ON A FLOURED WORK SURFACE for about 5 minutes. Return it to the bowl, cover with a tea towel and leave to rise for 30 minutes at room temperature.

TO MAKE THE FILLING, mix the butter, sugar and cinnamon together.

DIVIDE THE DOUGH IN HALF and roll it out to give two rectangles measuring 40 x 30cm. Spread the cinnamon filling over the top of each. Roll each piece of dough into a wide cylinder and cut into 1.5cm slices.

LINE SOME BAKING TRAYS WITH BAKING PAPER. Lay the cinnamon rolls on the paper, pressing down on each one so that they spread slightly. Cover and leave to rise for 20 minutes.

PREHEAT THE OVEN to 220°C (Gas 7). Brush the cinnamon rolls with the beaten egg and sprinkle with sugar. Bake for 12–15 minutes, then leave to cool on a wire rack. Serve warm or cold with a nice cup of tea.

Hot apple drink with Calvados *(Serves 4)*

1kg apples such as Cox's
Orange Pippins
100g caster sugar
1 litre water
1 long cinnamon stick plus
4 short cinnamon sticks
100ml Calvados
4 mint sprigs

CUT THE APPLES INTO FOUR WEDGES and place in a large saucepan with the sugar, water and long cinnamon stick. Bring to the boil, then reduce the heat and simmer for 30 minutes.

STRAIN THE APPLE-FLAVOURED LIQUID THROUGH A PIECE OF MUSLIN. Pour it back into the cleaned pan and bring to the boil. Add the Calvados and turn off the heat.

POUR INTO FOUR HEATPROOF GLASSES and serve each with a short cinnamon stick and a mint sprig.

November

Winter has started in the north. Some areas are already covered in snow. In the south it is dark and there is no snow to light up the landscape. The days are shorter and you spend most of your time indoors with candles lit and fire in the fireplace. It is time for soup, pheasant, Sunday roast and luxury cakes.

Soup is perfect for everyday meals or as a starter. This one has a creamy taste and grilled scallops soaked in lemon complement it nicely.

Cauliflower soup with grilled scallops *(Serves 4)*

SOUP

2 tbsp olive oil
1 onion, chopped
2 garlic cloves, chopped
2 tbsp curry powder
1 large cauliflower, chopped
1 litre water
100ml double cream
salt and pepper

SCALLOPS

12 scallops
2 tbsp olive oil
juice of ½ lemon
8 watercress sprigs

HEAT THE OIL IN A LARGE SAUCEPAN. Add the onion, garlic and curry powder and fry lightly. Add the cauliflower and water and bring to the boil, then reduce the heat and simmer for 30 minutes.

BRUSH THE SCALLOPS WITH OLIVE OIL and sprinkle with salt and freshly ground pepper. Heat a ridged grill pan and cook for 3 minutes on each side. Take the scallops off the heat and pour some lemon juice over them.

BLEND THE SOUP UNTIL SMOOTH in a blender or food processor, add the cream and season to taste with salt and pepper. Arrange the scallops on four skewers and serve on the top of the soup, decorated with watercress.

Scandinavia is experiencing a beer revolution and the many different flavours of beer now available are very exciting. Many of these beers are good to use in cooking. The following recipe uses brown ale to marinate pork cheeks.

Pork cheeks in brown ale *(Serves 8)*

2kg pork cheeks
750ml brown ale or similar dark beer
1 tbsp coriander seeds
1 tbsp whole peppercorns
3 tbsp olive oil
10 sprigs thyme
salt and pepper
600g potatoes, peeled and thickly sliced
3 carrots, peeled and thickly sliced
3 turnips, peeled and thickly sliced

IN A GLASS OR CERAMIC BOWL, marinate the meat in the brown ale, coriander seeds and peppercorns for 12 hours or overnight.

NEXT DAY, REMOVE THE PORK FROM THE MARINADE. Heat some olive oil in a casserole and brown the meat on all sides. Add the liquid from the marinade, then the thyme and some salt. Reduce the heat and leave to simmer for 1 hour.

ADD THE POTATOES TO THE CASSEROLE and leave to simmer for 15 minutes, then add the carrots and turnips and continue cooking for another 15 minutes. Season with salt and freshly ground pepper, then serve just as it is – the taste is very full and aromatic.

Pheasant can be tender and delicious, especially if you cook it with perfection and love. On Saturday nights in the autumn I like to cook pheasant, barded with good quality organic bacon and stuffed with bread and herbs, for close friends and family. When dinner is ready and the guests have arrived, I fetch some of my best red wine from the cellar and enjoy the pleasures of living in a part of the world were there are four very different seasons.

Braised stuffed pheasant with Savoy cabbage, gravy and potatoes *(Serves 4)*

2 pheasants
12 bacon rashers
300ml red wine
2 shallots, sliced
1 carrot, sliced
10 thyme sprigs
1 tablespoon whole
peppercorns
50ml port wine
300ml water
200ml double cream

STUFFING
2 slices bread, chopped
50g flat-leafed parsley
20 juniper berries, crushed

VEGETABLES
800g fingerling potatoes
salt and pepper
20–25g butter
200g hazelnuts, chopped
1 small Savoy cabbage, shredded

PREHEAT THE OVEN to 200°C (Gas 6). To make the stuffing, mix the bread and parsley with the juniper berries. Use this mixture to stuff the cavity of the pheasants.

WRAP THE BACON RASHERS AROUND THE BIRDS, pour over the red wine and roast in the oven for 15 minutes. Reduce the heat to 180°C (Gas 4), add the shallots, carrot, thyme, peppercorns, port wine and water. Tightly cover the tray with a sheet of foil and continue roasting for 35 minutes.

REMOVE THE PHEASANTS FROM THE OVEN again, discard the foil and stir in the cream. Return the pheasants to the oven for a final 20 minutes roasting.

MEANWHILE, BOIL THE POTATOES IN A LARGE PAN of salted water until tender, then drain. Once they are cool enough to handle, peel them. Keep warm until serving.

MELT THE BUTTER IN A FRYING PAN and sauté the chopped hazelnuts for a couple of minutes. Add the cabbage and 50ml water and fry for a few minutes more.

CARVE THE PHEASANTS and season the sauce to taste with salt and pepper. Serve the chunky vegetable sauce with the pheasant, cabbage and potatoes.

Moose is eaten during the hunting season. The meat is darkly red and can be used for various dishes such as hamburgers, stews and tournedos. Traditional cowberry compote (see page 84) is a perfect match. If you can't buy moose, venison is a good substitute.

Moose tournedos with kale salad and cowberry compote *(Serves 4)*

30g butter
4 tbsp olive oil
4 moose tournedos
100g chanterelles or other mushrooms
cowberry compote (page 84), to serve

SALAD
200g fresh kale, finely shredded
2 carrots, peeled and cut into thin batons
2 dessert apples, peeled, cored and cubed
2 tbsp walnut oil or vegetable oil
2 tbsp balsamic vinegar
salt and pepper

BALSAMIC ALMONDS
100g blanched almonds
1 tbsp honey
2 tbsp balsamic vinegar

TO START THE SALAD, mix the kale, carrots and apples in a bowl.

TOAST THE ALMONDS IN A HOT DRY FRYING PAN, stirring constantly so that they do not burn. When lightly browned and fragrant, add the honey and let it caramelize. Add the balsamic vinegar and simmer until the liquid has evaporated. Set the almonds aside to cool on a piece of baking paper, then chop them and add to the kale salad together with the oil and the balsamic vinegar. Season the salad with salt and freshly ground pepper.

IN A FRYING PAN, heat the butter and 2 tablespoons of the olive oil and fry the tournedos for 5–6 minutes on each side. Meanwhile, clean the chanterelles with a dry brush. Remove the tournedos from the frying pan and set aside to rest. Add the remaining oil to the frying pan and cook the mushrooms for 5 minutes.

SERVE WITH MOOSE TOURNEDOS WITH THE CHANTERELLES ON TOP and the salad and cowberry compote on the side.

This is one of very few dishes that my son and daughter, who normally disagree strongly on food, both claim as a favourite. It is filling and makes a nourishing family dinner when darkness is approaching, the rain is pouring down and the temperature is getting colder and colder. This recipe will serve a family of four for two evenings.

Meatballs in curry sauce *(Serves 8)*

MEATBALLS

500g minced pork

500g minced veal

1 small onion, chopped

2 garlic cloves, crushed

200ml milk

50g plain wheat flour

1 tbsp curry powder

5 tsp salt

pepper

4 eggs

2 bay leaves

SAUCE

30g butter

2 onions, chopped

2 garlic cloves, chopped

2 tbsp curry powder

2 tbsp plain wheat flour

200ml double cream

1 leek, sliced

2 carrots, peeled and cut into large chunks

2 apples, cored and sliced

COMBINE THE MINCED MEATS, ONION AND GARLIC IN A BOWL. Add the milk, flour, curry powder, 2 teaspoons of the salt and some freshly ground pepper and mix together. Add the eggs and mix again for about 5 minutes so that the mixture is as light and fluffy as possible.

HEAT 4–5 LITRES WATER IN A POT. Add the bay leaves and the remaining salt to the water and bring to the boil. Meanwhile, use your hands to shape half the meat mixture into little balls about 2cm wide. Plop them in the water and let them simmer for 20 minutes.

REMOVE THE MEATBALLS FROM THE BROTH WITH A SKIMMER AND PLACE ON A TRAY. Shape and cook the other half of the meat mixture in the same way. Set all the meatballs aside until the sauce is done, reserving 800ml of the cooking liquid.

IN ANOTHER POT, MELT THE BUTTER, add the onions, garlic and curry powder and cook for a couple of minutes. Add the flour and stir well. Add 100ml of the meatball cooking liquid and stir until smooth. Pour in the rest of the cooking liquid and bring to a simmer.

ADD THE CREAM AND RETURN TO THE BOIL. Reduce the heat, add the meatballs, leek and carrots and simmer for 5 minutes. Add the apples and continue cooking for 3 minutes. Season to taste with salt and pepper and serve with rice.

Sunday lunch is popular all over the Western world. It is an old tradition that families meet after church to eat their best meal of the week. Meat is, therefore, an essential part of the tradition because we used not to eat meat every day. One cannot claim that church plays a big part in people's lives nowadays, and many traditions have changed in tandem with changes in the way we live our lives, but Sunday lunch is nice and I think we should fight to maintain this tradition.

Old-fashioned roast with potatoes and scorzonera (Serves 8)

1 boneless ox roast, about 4kg
2 tbsp coarse sea salt
pepper
5 shallots, peeled and halved
3 carrots, peeled and roughly chopped
5 garlic cloves
3 rosemary sprigs
500ml red wine
500ml water

SAUCE
20g butter
2 garlic cloves, chopped
300g mushrooms, cut into wedges
1 tbsp plain wheat flour
150ml double cream

VEGETABLES
2kg potatoes
1kg scorzonera
milk, for soaking
4 tbsp olive oil

PREHEAT THE OVEN to 220°C (Gas 7). Trim any excess fat from the bottom of the joint. Score a diamond pattern in the top layer of fat and sprinkle with the coarse salt and some freshly ground pepper. Place the roast in a large roasting tin. Arrange the shallots, carrots, garlic and rosemary around the meat and roast for 15 minutes.

LOWER THE OVEN TEMPERATURE to 180°C (Gas 4) and add the red wine and water to the tin. Continue roasting for 1 hour and 45 minutes, adding a bit more water now and then, so it does not dry out.

WHEN DONE, TAKE THE ROAST FROM THE TIN AND SET ASIDE TO REST. Strain the pan juices into a glass bowl and leave to stand until the broth and fat separate. Discard the fat. Measure the broth and, if there is not 600ml, add some water.

BOIL THE POTATOES IN A LARGE PAN OF SALTED WATER, then peel them and keep warm until serving time. Meanwhile, peel the scorzonera and soak in milk to prevent discolouration.

TO MAKE THE SAUCE, melt the butter in a saucepan, add the garlic and mushrooms and cook for 2 minutes. Add the flour and stir well. Add the broth and bring to the boil, then reduce the heat and simmer for 10 minutes, before adding the cream and simmering for another 5 minutes. Season to taste with salt and pepper.

HEAT THE OLIVE OIL IN A FRYING PAN and fry the scorzonera for 5 minutes, then season with salt and pepper. Carve the meat and serve with the sauce, potatoes and scorzonera.

Known as medals, these very popular cakes are served for afternoon coffee. They are crisp and creamy, sweet and fresh.

Medaljer *(Makes 10)*

PASTRY

200g plain wheat flour
50g icing sugar
1 tsp organic lemon zest
100g chilled butter, chopped
½ beaten egg

FILLING

½ vanilla pod
2 apples such as Cox's Orange Pippin, peeled, cored and cubed
100g demerara sugar
200ml double cream

TOPPING

200g good-quality dark chocolate
40g butter

TO MAKE THE PASTRY, sift the flour and icing sugar in to a mixing bowl and add the lemon zest. Rub the butter into the dry ingredients until the mixture resembles breadcrumbs. Add the egg and stir until the pastry comes together in a ball. Wrap in cling film and chill for 30 minutes.

PREHEAT THE OVEN to 220°C (Gas 7) and line a baking tray with baking paper. Roll out the pastry on a floured work surface to a thickness of 2–3mm. Use a 6–7cm-diameter pastry cutter or the rim of a glass to cut the pastry into discs. Spread them out on the baking paper and bake for 6–7 minutes, then transfer carefully (they are a bit fragile) to a wire rack to cool.

CUT THE HALF VANILLA POD LENGTHWAYS and scape the seeds out with the tip of a knife. Put the apples in a saucepan with the sugar and the vanilla seeds and bring to the boil, then reduce the heat and leave to simmer for 20 minutes. Stir the apple mixture together to give a thick sauce, then leave to cool.

MELT THE CHOCOLATE AND BUTTER TOGETHER IN A DOUBLE BOILER and stir until smooth. Spread half the pastry discs (medals) with the chocolate mixture, leaving a 2mm border. Put aside to let the chocolate set. These are the 'upper medals'.

WHIP THE CREAM UNTIL IT FORMS STIFF PEAKS. Take the remaining medals and place one teaspoon of apple sauce on each. Fit a piping bag with a star-shaped nozzle and fill with whipped cream. Pipe a ring of cream around the apple sauce. These are the 'lower medals'.

PUT THE 'UPPER MEDALS' ON TOP OF THE 'LOWER MEDALS' so that they cover the apple sauce and whipped cream. Serve immediately with coffee or tea.

December

In Scandinavia we celebrate Christmas on the evening of December 24th. If you go to church, you do so in the afternoon. After a very rich meal you are so full you cannot move, so of course you have to dance around the Christmas tree, which must be lit with real candles. Some families are more dedicated to carols than others. Finally, we open presents and have coffee, Danish butter cookies, homemade chocolates, oranges and apples. It is a long but delightful evening if you happen to love Christmas, as I do.

SUNDAYS IN ADVENT. The four Sundays before Christmas are called 'Sundays in advent'. Many people will throw an afternoon party on one of these Sundays, get together to bake cookies, make gingerbread houses, go skating, take a walk in the woods, play games, eat Christmas doughnuts (æbleskiver) and drink mulled wine. The butter-fried doughnuts are cooked in a special pan that has about 10 ball-like indentations, but you could simply fry them like pancakes. Glögg is warm red wine with aquavit and spices. It is a lovely drink to serve when it is cold outside. Be careful with the aquavit, or leave it out altogether, to make the mulled wine a bit lighter, with a sweeter taste.

Christmas doughnuts (Serves 10–12)

40g fresh yeast
800ml lukewarm milk
550g plain wheat flour
2 tsp salt
1½ tsp ground cardamom
2 vanilla pods
2 tbsp caster sugar
4 eggs, separated
100–150g butter, for frying

TO SERVE
icing sugar
raspberry jam

DISSOLVE THE YEAST IN THE MILK IN A BOWL. In another mixing bowl, sift together the flour, salt and cardamom. Slit the vanilla pods lengthways, scrape out the seeds with the tip of a knife and add them to the dry ingredients with the sugar.

WHISK THE EGG YOLKS INTO THE MILK MIXTURE – using an electric mixer if possible. Add the dry ingredients and beat to make a dough. In a separate bowl, whisk the egg whites until stiff, then fold them into the dough. Leave the batter to stand for 40 minutes.

HEAT THE PAN OVER A MEDIUM HEAT. Put a little butter in each indentation and when it has melted pour in some of the batter. Cook for 3–5 minutes or until golden underneath, then turn the doughnuts over so that they form a ball. Continue frying for about 5 minutes, then remove from the pan and repeat with the remaining batter.

DUST WITH ICING SUGAR and serve immediately with raspberry jam and hot mulled wine

Mulled wine (Serves 8)

500ml water
1 cinnamon stick, smashed
1 tbsp whole cloves
1 tbsp dried orange zest (pommeran)
1 tbsp coarsely chopped cardamom pods
2 bottles red wine
4 tbsp caster sugar
600ml aquavit or vodka (optional)
200g raisins
200g blanched almonds, chopped

PUT THE WATER IN A SAUCEPAN with the cinnamon stick, cloves, dried orange zest and cardamom pods and bring it slowly to the boil. Reduce the heat and simmer for 15 minutes, then turn the heat off and leave to stand for another 15 minutes before draining the mixture through a sieve. Discard the spices and save the liquid.

IN A SAUCEPAN, combine the spiced liquid, red wine and sugar and bring slowly to the boil, then reduce the heat and simmer for 10 minutes.

ADD THE AQUAVIT OR VODKA, if using, the raisins and almonds and simmer gently for 5 minutes, but do not let it boil. If you prefer a sweeter drink, add more sugar. Serve in tall glasses with spoons so that you can catch the raisins and almonds.

Legend has it that on 13 December 1764 a gentleman in Sweden was roused in the middle of the night by a beautiful voice. He saw a young woman in white moving through his room singing. She had wings and was carrying a candle. That was Lucia the Saint. She brought light, food and wine as comfort on what was, in the Gregorian calendar, the longest night of the year. We celebrate that on 13th December. Children will walk with lit candles singing the beautiful Lucia carol and bringing the Lucia bread.

Swedish Lucia bread *(Makes 22)*

40g yeast
500ml lukewarm milk
5g saffron
200g butter, melted
1kg plain wheat flour
1 tsp salt
100g caster sugar
50g raisins

TO FINISH
44 raisins
1 egg, beaten

DISSOLVE THE YEAST IN THE WARM MILK in a mixing bowl, then add the saffron and keep stirring until the mixture turns yellow. Add the melted butter. In a separate mixing bowl, sift together the flour and salt, then stir in the sugar and raisins.

POUR THE YEAST MIXTURE INTO THE DRY INGREDIENTS AND STIR until the dough comes cleanly from the edge of the bowl. Knead the dough on a floured work surface for 10 minutes, until it is shiny but not sticky. Put the dough back in the bowl and leave to rise for 1½ hours at room temperature.

LIGHTLY KNEAD THE DOUGH AGAIN ON A FLOURED WORK SURFACE. Divide it into 22 equal pieces. Roll them into sausages then curl the ends so that each piece is shaped like the number 8. Put one raisin in the middle of each circle. Place the breads on baking trays lined with baking paper, cover with tea towels and leave to rise again for 30 minutes.

PREHEAT THE OVEN to 180°C (Gas 4). Brush the risen breads with beaten egg and bake for 20–25 minutes or until golden brown all over, then remove from the oven and leave to cool on a wire rack. Eat them as they are, or spread with cold butter.

Pork foreloin or 'pork roast' is one of the most popular cuts of meat in Scandinavia, though this traditional cut is not as well known as it once was in Britain. Serve it with the crisp pork rind on top. The Waldorf salad is sweet and crisp and goes well with pork.

Pork with rosemary, thyme and garlic *(Serves 6)*

1 organic lemon
3 rosemary sprigs
5 thyme sprigs
5 garlic cloves, finely chopped
salt and pepper
2.5kg pork foreloin

PREHEAT THE OVEN to 200°C (Gas 6). Grate the zest from the lemon, then cut the lemon in half and slice it finely. In a mixing bowl, combine the zest, lemon slices, rosemary, thyme, garlic, salt and freshly ground pepper.

REMOVE THE PORK RIND IN ONE PIECE from the top of the roast, making sure that the fat stays underneath the rind. Score a diamond pattern on the top surface of the pork, then rub in the herb-lemon mixture. Put the piece of rind and fat back on top. Tie all the way along the joint with a long piece of kitchen string, then place it in a roasting tin and roast for 1 hour 40 minutes.

REMOVE THE PORK FROM THE OVEN and leave to rest for about 15 minutes so that the juices can settle throughout the meat, then remove the string and carve it into slices, making sure there is a piece of the crisp pork rind with every portion. If it is Christmas Eve, serve it with the traditional roast duck and duck gravy (see page 212), with caramel potatoes and red cabbage (see page 214).

Waldorf salad *(Serves 6)*

200g green grapes, halved and deseeded
100g walnuts, broken into bits
2 apples, cored and cubed
100ml double cream

PUT THE GRAPES, WALNUTS AND APPLES in a mixing bowl and stir.

IN A SEPARATE BOWL, whip the cream until it forms soft peaks then fold it into the salad. Serve as soon as possible.

You could eat this ham on Christmas Eve, or for Christmas lunch, when it would be part of a large buffet with herrings, salads and potatoes. The ham could also serve as a roast with different salads, bread and cheese. It goes well with the autumn salads on page 176.

Swedish Christmas ham *(Serves 15 as part of a buffet)*

3kg ham, either on the bone or boned and rolled

PLACE THE HAM IN LARGE BOWL, cover with cold water and leave to soak for 12 hours.

4 litres water

PREHEAT THE OVEN to 130°C (Gas ½). Put the ham in a large roasting tray, add the water and slowly roast in the oven for about 3 hours and 15 minutes, until a meat thermometer inserted in the ham reads 75°C.

GLAZE
2 egg yolks
50g breadcrumbs
150g wholegrain mustard
100g dark brown sugar
pepper

MIX TOGETHER ALL THE GLAZE INGREDIENTS IN A BOWL. Remove the ham from the oven and leave it to cool slightly. Raise the oven temperature to 220°C (Gas 7).

REMOVE THE RIND FROM THE HAM and score a diamond pattern in the top layer of fat. Brush the glaze over the ham and return to the oven. Roast for 10 minutes or until the ham is golden brown. Leave to cool before serving.

CHRISTMAS DINNER. This is a lovely meal that you could serve on other days of the year as well. For my family's Christmas dinner, I also cook the roast pork with Waldorf salad (see page 208), and serve with redcurrant jelly. It is a real feast.

Roast duck *(Serves 4)*

1 free-range duck
salt and pepper

PREHEAT THE OVEN to 200°C (Gas 6). Pour boiling water over the duck. Rub the inside of the duck with salt and freshly ground pepper. Mix the apple and prunes together, put them in the cavity then close it with a trussing needle. Season the outside with salt and pepper.

FILLING
1 apple, such as Cox's Orange Pippin, cored and cubed
100g prunes

PLACE THE DUCK ON A RACK and place the rack in a roasting tray. Roast for 2½ hours, then leave the duck to rest for 10 minutes. Raise the oven temperature to 230°C (Gas 8).

CARVE THE DUCK INTO TEN PIECES, place in an ovenproof dish and return to the oven for 10 minutes. Serve the duck with the apple-prune mixture on the side.

Gravy *(Serves 4)*

DUCK STOCK
2 duck legs
750ml red wine
1 litre water
1 carrot
1 onion, unpeeled
10 thyme sprigs
1 tbsp whole peppercorns
1 tbsp coarse salt

TO MAKE THE STOCK, fry the duck legs in a large saucepan, turning occasionally, until they are golden brown. Add the red wine, water, carrot, onion, thyme, peppercorns and salt. Bring to the boil, then reduce the heat and leave to simmer for 2 hours, or up to 4 hours if you have time.

STRAIN THE STOCK USING A SIEVE and discard the duck and vegetables. Pour the broth into a container and leave to cool, then cover and store in the refrigerator overnight. Before use, scrape all the duck fat from the surface and save it for cooking the red cabbage (recipe overleaf).

GRAVY
50g butter
2 tbsp plain wheat flour
800ml duck stock
300ml double cream
2 tsp redcurrant jelly
1 tsp gravy browning (optional)
salt and pepper

TO MAKE THE GRAVY, melt the butter in a saucepan. Add the flour and stir until the paste comes away from the edge of the pan. Add the stock a little at a time, stirring after each addition until there are no lumps left. Bring the stock slowly to a simmer, stirring constantly.

STIR IN THE CREAM, redcurrant jelly and gravy browning (if using). Season to taste with salt and freshly ground pepper and keep warm until ready to serve.

This may seem an unusual way of cooking potatoes, but as far as my children and I are concerned, Christmas isn't Christmas without caramel potatoes. Another essential side dish is red cabbage. Its wonderful sweet-sour-spicy flavour goes well with duck. I think the taste improves when red cabbage is prepared the day before serving.

Caramel potatoes *(Serves 4–6)*

1kg baby potatoes
150g caster sugar
90g butter

BOIL THE POTATOES IN A LARGE PAN of salted water until tender, then drain. Once they are cool enough to handle, peel them and leave to cool (this can be done the day before serving).

SHORTLY BEFORE SERVING CHRISTMAS DINNER, melt the sugar in a large sauté pan. When it is golden brown, add the butter and let the mixture simmer until it becomes a caramel, stirring as little as possible.

ADD THE POTATOES and gently turn them in the caramel until it starts to stick to them – this will take time, so be patient.

Red cabbage *(Serves 4–6)*

4 tbsp duck fat
½ red cabbage, cored and thinly sliced
1 whole yellow onion
200ml red wine
100g caster sugar
1 cinnamon stick
10 whole cloves
4 tbsp redcurrant jelly
50ml vinegar or brine from pickled beetroots
salt and pepper

MELT THE DUCK FAT IN A LARGE SAUCEPAN OR CASSEROLE, add the cabbage and fry it over a medium heat until shiny – don't let it brown.

ADD THE REMAINING INGREDIENTS and season with salt and freshly ground pepper. Cover and leave to simmer for 2 hours. Remove the onion and season to taste with sugar, salt and pepper.

This is my favourite pudding for Christmas Eve. When serving it, you also play a little Christmas game. The rice pudding is served in a large bowl. Just before you take it to the table, add one whole almond and stir so nobody knows where it is. Everybody eats until someone finds the almond. You are allowed to cheat and hide the almond from the others if you find it, because the point of the game is to make the others keep eating while trying to find the almond. In the end, when a person can no longer hide that he or she has the almond, the person receives a present. Make the rice pudding and the cherry sauce the day before serving.

Rice pudding with warm cherry sauce *(Serves 6)*

RICE PUDDING
1.4 litres organic whole milk
2 vanilla pods
250g short grain pudding rice
1 tsp salt
2 tbsp caster sugar
150g blanched almonds
200ml double cream

CHERRY SAUCE
700g pitted cherries, fresh, frozen or in brine
200g caster sugar
1 vanilla pod
500ml water
3 tbsp cornflour

GENTLY HEAT **1.3** LITRES OF THE MILK in a large saucepan. Slit one of the vanilla pods lengthways, without cutting it all the way through. Just before the milk starts to boil, add the rice and the slit vanilla pod. Cook gently for 30 minutes, stirring slowly and frequently so that it doesn't burn. Remove the pan from the heat and add the salt. Cover and leave for 10 minutes. Remove the lid, stir in the sugar and leave to cool (or until the next day).

REMOVE THE VANILLA POD and transfer the rice mixture to a large bowl. Chop the almonds coarsely except for one, which you save for the game. Whip the cream in a bowl until it forms soft peaks. Slit the second vanilla pod lengthways and scrape out the seeds with the tip of a knife. Add them to the rice. Gently fold in the remaining milk, then fold in one-third of the whipped cream. When the mixture is smooth, fold in the rest of the whipped cream and the chopped almonds. Taste the pudding: it should be sweet with a flavour of vanilla. Spoon the pudding into a serving bowl and hide the almond. Cover and place the bowl in the refrigerator.

TO MAKE THE CHERRY SAUCE, put the fruit in a saucepan with the sugar, vanilla pod and water. Bring to the boil, then reduce the heat and simmer for 15 minutes. Dissolve the cornflour in enough water to make a thin paste and slowly add it into the cherry sauce, stirring constantly until it thickens and comes slowly to the boil. Taste and add some more sugar if necessary but do not make it too sweet because the rice pudding is very sweet and the cherry sauce should add some acidity to it.

SHORTLY BEFORE you are going to serve the rice pudding, reheat the sauce and serve it on the side in a bowl.

SMÅKAGER: CHRISTMAS COOKIES. Vanilla butter cookies are the best in the world – crisp with the taste of real vanilla – and the swirl cookies have the added taste of chocolate. Be sure to make enough to last the entire Christmas holidays! The marzipan nougat delights are easy to make with children. Try cutting them into different shapes and covering them in chocolate.

Crisp vanilla Danish butter cookies *(Makes 80)*

375g butter
250g caster sugar
1 egg
2 vanilla pods
500g plain wheat flour

CREAM THE BUTTER AND SUGAR TOGETHER IN A BOWL until the mixture is pale and fluffy. Add the egg and continue beating. Split the vanilla pods lengthways and scrape out the seeds with the tip of a knife. Stir them into the flour, then fold all the dry ingredients into the butter mixture. Wrap in cling film and chill for 2 hours.

PREHEAT THE OVEN to 200°C (Gas 6). Roll the dough into very thin sausages about 5 or 6cm long. Curl each one into a ring and press the ends firmly together. Place on a baking tray lined with baking paper. Bake for about 8 minutes, then cool on a wire rack. Store the cookies in an airtight tin and do not mix them with other types of cookies or they will go soft.

Swirl butter cookies *(Makes 120)*

300g butter
150g icing sugar
1 egg
400g plain wheat flour
75g cocoa powder
1 egg, beaten

CREAM THE BUTTER AND ICING SUGAR TOGETHER with an electric mixer until the mixture is pale and fluffy. Add the egg and beat well, then stir in the flour. Divide the dough in half and add the cocoa to one portion, working it until fully combined.

PREHEAT THE OVEN to 200°C (Gas 6). Roll both pieces of dough out into rectangles. Brush the pale dough with some of the beaten egg then cover it with the chocolate dough. Starting from the longest side, roll up the dough to form a cylinder with a swirl pattern inside.

CUT THE CYLINDER INTO THIN SLICES and put them on a baking tray lined with baking paper. Glaze with the rest of the egg and bake for 8 minutes or until golden brown, then remove from the oven and cool on a wire rack.

Marzipan nougat delights *(Makes 45–50)*

400g marzipan (page 72)
icing sugar, to dust
200g soft nougat

CUT THE MARZIPAN IN THREE and roll out one piece on a work surface dusted with icing sugar until the marzipan is about 5mm thick. Halve the soft nougat and roll out one piece on top of the rolled marzipan to cover it.

ROLL OUT THE SECOND PIECE OF MARZIPAN as before and lay it on top of the nougat, followed by the remaining nougat. Roll out the final piece of marzipan and lay it over the stack so that you end up with a total of five layers alternating marzipan and nougat.

CUT INTO SMALL DIAMOND SHAPES and serve, or store in an airtight box and eat within 3 days.

Glossary

AQUAVIT. This traditional Scandinavian alcohol can be made from potatoes or grains, depending on which is most economical. The choice does not have any influence on the taste, the taste is the result of the herbs and berries that are added. Aquavit is served in specially designed glasses with lunch or dinner. The most famous brands are Line Aquavit (Norway), Rød Aalborg and Jubilæum (Denmark), and OP Anderson (Sweden). In Denmark we also have a new upmarket brand called Schumacher. Many Scandinavians still make their own aquavit with a variety of herbs and berries.

BEER. A wide range of beer is produced in Scandinavia. In the last ten years numerous so-called microbreweries have opened in the region. They bring new and exciting flavours to beer. Carlsberg has also developed a special range of beers named after IP Jacobsen, the founder of the company. They taste very nice and are perfect with marinated meat or poultry.

BEETROOT. This root vegetable can be round or cylindrical and is available in both summer and winter varieties. Beetroot have a sweet taste and are commonly preserved and served as a condiment with meat dishes. However, they are also good baked and eaten raw in salads.

BUTTERMILK. When milk and cream are churned, the fat separates from the milk. The fat is then used to make butter and the remaining liquid is buttermilk. It has the fresh taste of green fields. Buttermilk is very useful for baking and makes a healthy drink that is delicious served cold.

CARAWAY SEEDS. This tiny dark coloured seed looks like cumin but has a very different taste.

In Scandinavia caraway seeds are typically used in aquavit, bread and cheese; I also use them in salads and stews.

CARDAMOM. The Swedes traditionally use this spice in cakes, buns and bread, but also in minced meat mixtures. It is available ground, but I prefer to buy the green pods and grind them just before use.

COWBERRIES. Very small red berries, rather like small cranberries, cowberries grow wild on bushes in the woods and are picked in late summer or early autumn. They are very sour and have a very high vitamin C content. Cowberries are traditionally made into cordial, or boiled with sugar to make lingonsylt – in Sweden it is a must to have lingonsylt with your meatballs.

CRÈME FRAÎCHE. Scandinavians learned to use this type of soured cream from the French. It is often served with cakes and tarts and used in dressings and cold sauces. In Scandinavia crème fraîche is available in various different fat levels from nine to 38 per cent fat.

HAM. In Scandinavia cured ham is soaked in water then either baked or boiled. When served for dinner it is often baked with a marinade made of brown sugar and mustard. Different cuts of pork are used for ham in different parts of Scandinavia, some with the bone, others boneless.

HERRING. Herrings live in cold, salty water. For thousands of years in Scandinavia herrings has been both basic food and served for more festive occasions. When caught they are salted and stored in large sealed buckets so that they last a long time. When you want to eat them you soak them in water to remove the salt. You can also eat fresh herring fillets fried in butter, and buy them smoked, but the most common way to enjoy herrings in Scandinavia is marinated.

HORSERADISH. Horseradish is a long root that grows underground. You can buy it fresh and grate it yourself, or buy it ready-grated. Preserved horseradish is fine for dressings and sauces. When you are lucky enough to have a fresh root, wrap some of it in cling film and store it in the fridge; it is best grated just before cooking or eating.

JERUSALEM ARTICHOKES. A winter root vegetable, Jerusalem artichokes have a nutty taste and are very crunchy when eaten raw. They are suitable for salads, soups, and can be served baked or boiled.

LOVAGE. Lovage is a herb grown in Scandinavian gardens year-round. It has a very sharp taste and needs to be used judiciously. Salads, dressings, chicken stews and garnishing are some of its best uses and, unlike some other herbs, lovage does not lose its flavour when cooked.

MARZIPAN. The quality of marzipan depends on the quantity of almonds it contains. Look for marzipan with an almond content of at least 60 per cent; the colour should be golden instead of white, and the texture should be soft and shiny. If you cannot get hold of good quality marzipan, you can always make it yourself.

MUSTARD. Many different kinds of mustard are enjoyed in Scandinavia. We have one for fish sauces which is grainy and has a sweet taste, another variety is more like Dijon mustard – very strong and a bit sour. Whole mustard seeds are also used for preserves and marinated herrings.

OILS AND FATS. When cooking I mostly use olive oil and butter, for both taste and health reasons. When baking, it has to be butter to get the best result and flavour, but for frying I very rarely use butter and instead choose olive oil or some other kind of vegetable oil. I also favour olive oil for making salad dressings and marinades.

POTATOES. Potatoes are very important in the Scandinavian diet and can be eaten for almost every hot meal. Many different kinds are grown in different parts of the region. New potatoes are very popular and harvested around midsummer. They are best boiled within 24 hours of being harvested, and on those occasions should be eaten with cold butter and salt only.

POTATO FLOUR. Starch derived from potatoes and made into a flour in a very complicated chemical process. In Scandinavia it is widely used both for baking and thickening sauces. Often cornflour can be used in its place.

REDCURRANTS. Small red berries that grow in small clusters on bushes both wild and in gardens. In season in Scandinavia in July and August, redcurrants have a fresh, sweet taste but can be a bit sour. They are eaten fresh on cakes and in fruit salads, or shaken with sugar to eat in the morning. Redcurrants are also made into jellies and lemonade right after picking.

RYE FLOUR. Flour made from rye grains. I prefer to buy rye flour from small organic producers. It should not be more than two months old, even if the packet says the flour can last up to a year.

RYE BREADS. The foundation of the famous open sandwich, these loaves have rye flour as their main ingredient. In Scandinavia they are often made with sourdough culture. Honey, malt flour and different grains can be added to vary the flavour and texture.

SALMON. Salmon lives in both salty and fresh water. It is a fatty fish yet very firm, easy to handle and cook. It has become part of our everyday kitchen. You can eat it raw, marinated, fried, gravad ('buried'), or smoked. When you buy fresh salmon check that the colour is bright, the smell is fresh, and that the surface of the flesh is clean and not slimy.

SOURDOUGH CULTURE. Used for traditional rye breads in particular. In Scandinavia sourdough culture can be bought ready-made in specialist shops and health food stores, but you can also make it yourself, either from yeast or baking ferment.

SPELT. This ancient grain dates back to the Roman Empire and is related to wheat. The flour is popular in Scandinavia because it has a very nice taste, is easy to work with and perfect for bread and buns.

TROUT. If I want to steam a fish, rainbow trout from Norway is my favourite, and I prefer it to salmon. The meat is firm and tender with a fresh sweet taste. I recommend buying and cooking it whole, rather than in fillets.

VINEGARS. We generally use a plain, clear spirit vinegar for brines and to enhance the flavour of dishes when cooking. It is also used for housekeeping tasks such as cleaning and stain removal.

YEAST. Fresh yeast is a staple in Scandinavian supermarkets. Baking is still part of daily life in many households, especially in the countryside. Even people who do not bake often will bake for birthdays and the Christmas festivities. Fresh yeast is favoured for pastry and cakes as well as bread. Dried yeast can be substituted, certainly, but I believe fresh yeast gives the best result.

YOGHURT. Scandinavia produces a wide range of different yoghurt products with varying fat contents. They are used for breakfast, drinking, snacking, and for making dressings and desserts.

WEBSITES WHERE YOU CAN FIND MORE INFORMATION ABOUT SCANDINAVIA AND ITS FOOD PRODUCTS

TRAVEL
www.sas.dk
www.drholms.no
www.visitcopenhagen.com
www.visitnorway.com
www.visitdenmark.com
www.visitsweden.com

AQUAVIT
www.schumachers.dk
www.distillers.dk
www.arcusbeverage.com

APPLES
www.kiviksmusteri.se

BEER
www.jacobsenbryg.dk
www.nogne-o.com
www.nilsoscar.se

CHEESE
www.st-clemens.dk
www.tine.no
www.loegismose.dk

RETAILERS (UK)
www.nordicbakery.com
www.scandikitchen.co.uk
www.totallyswedish.com

MISCELLANEOUS
www.royalcopenhagen.com
www.TrineHahnemann.com

Index

Acknowledgements

It has been a wonderful journey writing this book and I have a lot of people to thank for helping me make it happen. Firstly, an enormous thanks to Anne Furniss for taking on the project and for believing in me, and also to her and Helen Lewis for creative meetings and for being so responsive during 2007. Thanks also to all the other talented people at Quadrille. Thanks to Stig Jensen, the chef in Snapstinget, Copenhagen, and the staff there for wonderful and inspiring lunches served throughout the process.

Thanks to Lars Ranek for some wonderful trips around Scandinavia where we had a great time and where he took some beautiful pictures, and to Vibeke Kaupert for helping to put this book together.

I would also like to thank my mother for her support and a lot of hard work helping me in the kitchen with trying out recipes, and cleaning up after long days in the photographic studio! Also thanks to my friend Lisa Høgh Nielsen for helping me in the kitchen at all hours, to my soul mate in food Sonja Bock for going through my ideas, and my sister Silla Bjerrum for her encouragement and sharing her network.

Special thanks to Dr. Holms Hotel in Norway for their hospitality. Finally, thanks to my husband Niels Peter for wonderful support and for never really tiring of all the cooking, litter and cleaning up. Thanks for working with me into the long hours and for reading through drafts of the book again and again.